AnimalWays

Chimpanzees

AnimalWays

Chimpanzees

REBECCA STEFOFF

BENCHMARK BOOKS

MARSHALL CAVENDISH

NEW YORK

With thanks to Dr. Dan Wharton, director of the Central Park Wildlife Center, for his expert reading of this manuscript.

Benchmark Books
Marshall Cavendish
99 White Plains Road
Tarrytown, NY 10591-9001
www.marshallcavendish.com

Library of Congress Cataloging-in-Publication Data
Stefoff, Rebecca, 1951–
Chimpanzees / by Rebecca Stefoff.
v. cm. — (Animalways)
Includes bibliographical references and index.
Contents: "So much resembling man"—The chimpanzee family tree—Physical features—Life cycle—Behavior—Chimpanzees today and tomorrow.
ISBN 0-7614-1579-3
1. Chimpanzees—Juvenile literature. [1. Chimpanzees.] I. Title. II. Series.
QL737.P96S742   2003   599.885—dc21   2003002008

Photo Research by Candlepants Incorporated

Cover Photo: Corbis/Renne Lynn

The photographs in this book are used by permission and through the courtesy of: *Steve Bloom Images:* title page, 33, 35, 37, 45 (bottom), 46, 53, 57, 59, 65, 73, 76, 83, 84 (bottom), 87, 89, 99; *Corbis:* Karl Ammann: 2, 19, 61 (bottom), 64; George D. Lepp: 9; Tom Brakefield: 13, 63, 81; Henry Diltz, 14; Reuters NewMedia Inc., 23; Karen Huntt Mason, 28; Bettmann, 32, 95; Nigel J. Dennis/Gallo Images: 45 (top); Yann Arthur-Bertrand: 49, 50; Kennan Ward: 55, 61 (top), 79, 80; Martin Harvey/Gallo Images: 58, 70, 97; Tim Davis: 67; Gallo Images: 84 (top); Anna Clopet: 93; Carl & Ann Purcell: 100; Charles Krebs, 103. *Art Resource, NY:* Werner Forman: 11; *Photofest:* 16; 91; *Photo Researchers:* John Reader/Science Photo Library: 30.

Printed in China

1 3 5 6 4 2

Contents

Animal Kingdom

CNIDARIANS

coral

ARTHROPODS
(animals with jointed limbs and external skeleton)

MOLLUSKS

squid

CRUSTACEANS

crab

ARACHNIDS

spider

INSECTS

grasshopper

MYRIAPODS

centipede

CARNIVORES

lion

SEA MAMMALS

whale

PRIMATES

CHIMPANZEE

HERBIVORES
(5 orders)

elephant

PHYLA

ANNELIDS

earthworm

CHORDATES
(animals with
a dorsal
nerve chord)

ECHINODERMS

starfish

SUB PHYLA

VERTEBRATES
(animals with a
backbone)

CLASSES

FISH

fish

BIRDS

gull

MAMMALS

AMPHIBIANS

frog

REPTILES

snake

ORDERS

RODENTS

squirrel

INSECTIVORES

mole

MARSUPIALS

koala

SMALL MAMMALS
(several orders)

bat

1 "So Much Resembling Man"

At the beginning of the seventeenth century, an Englishman named Andrew Battell was held prisoner for a time in West Africa, a part of the world almost entirely unknown to Europeans. Battell returned to England in 1607 with stories of his adventures and the strange new creatures he had seen. Among other things, he described certain "Monsters, which are common . . . and very dangerous." Battell spoke of a monstrous creature that was "in all proportion like a man, but that he is more like a Giant in stature, than a man: for he is very tall, and hath a mans face, hollow eyed, with long haire upon his brows. His bodie is full of haire, but not very thicke, and it is of a dunnish colour. . . . They sleepe in the trees, and build shelters for the raine. They feed upon Fruit that they find in the Woods, and upon Nuts, for they eate no kind of flesh. They cannot speak, and have no understanding more than a beast."

In describing the creature that we now know as the chimpanzee, Battell made two important points. The creature is like

a man in various ways, but it is not a man. Even though Battell's creatures were shaped like human beings, they could not be human. Human beings communicate with language, but the African "monsters" did not have the gift of speech. To Battell this meant that their understanding of the world was that of a beast, or animal.

What would Battell think of Austin, a chimpanzee who typed the symbols for *funny face* on a special computer keyboard and then immediately stuck out his tongue and made a funny face? Or of the chimp Kanzi, who pressed the keyboard symbols for *Matata bite* after the first time his mother, Matata, disciplined him by giving him a nip with her teeth? Perhaps the seventeenth-century Englishman would be too puzzled by the computer to pay much attention to the chimpanzees. But perhaps he would wonder if the chimps had actually "spoken." Maybe he would begin to examine his ideas about language, intelligence, and the relationship between men and animals. Today, studies of chimpanzees in the wild and in the laboratory are casting light on these subjects and providing new information about the closest living relatives of human beings.

Early Encounters

Biologists classify both chimpanzees and human beings in the large group of mammals called primates. Apes are a subgroup of the primates. The siamangs and orangutans of Asia are apes, as are the gorillas, chimpanzees, and bonobos or pygmy chimpanzees of Africa. Monkeys are another primate subgroup, spread over a much larger part of the world than the apes. People in the Near East, the Mediterranean world, and Europe knew of monkeys long before they encountered apes. Baboons and other kinds of monkeys can still be seen in wall paintings

A TRADITIONAL SUBJECT IN ASIAN ART IS THREE MONKEYS ILLUSTRATING GOOD BEHAVIOR BY HEARING NO EVIL, SPEAKING NO EVIL, AND SEEING NO EVIL.

made by the ancient Egyptians more than four thousand years ago. The ancient Hebrews and Greeks were familiar with monkeys, too, and mentioned them in some of their writings.

The first Westerners to see an ape may have been seafarers from the ancient city of Carthage, in North Africa. According to some old texts, a Carthaginian captain named Hanno led a fleet out of the Mediterranean Sea and south along the western coast of Africa around 470 B.C. Somewhere along that coast, probably near the modern nation of Sierra Leone, the Carthaginians landed on an island where hairy, forest-dwelling creatures threw stones at them. The sailors captured and killed several of these animals, carrying their skins back to Carthage. According to the ancient Roman scholar Pliny the Elder, two of the skins remained in Carthage until Rome destroyed the city in 146 B.C. Most modern scholars think that the animals Hanno saw and captured were chimpanzees, which have been known to throw stones and sticks at their enemies.

Many centuries later, Europeans began exploring Africa south of the Sahara Desert. This brought them into the home of the chimpanzee. Encounters between these two species of primates—chimps and humans—became more and more common. Travelers like Andrew Battell told of the hairy, humanlike creatures that lived in the African forests. In 1640 the Prince of Orange, ruler of the Netherlands, received a present from Africa: the first live chimpanzee to reach Europe. The following year, a Dutch physician named Nicolaas Tulp published a scientific description of the animal. He called it an orang-outang, from an Asian word for "man of the woods." However, Tulp's subject was not the ape we now know as the orangutan, which comes from Asia. Instead, Tulp's ape came from Angola, on Africa's western coast, and was most likely a chimpanzee.

In 1699 a London scientist named Edward Tyson dissected the body of a captive chimp that had died. He described the chimpanzee (which he also called an orang-outang) in a 1699 book that compared the ape's anatomy, or physical structure, to those of a man and a monkey. Tyson wrote that the ape was "a sort of *Animal* so much resembling *Man*, that both the Ancients and the Moderns have reputed it to be a Puny Race of Mankind." Tyson, considered by some historians of science to be the founder of primatology, correctly saw that the chimpanzee has characteristics of both monkey and human and lies somewhere between them.

People have long been amused, fascinated, and sometimes disturbed by the fact that chimpanzees look and act so much like human beings. During the seventeenth and eighteenth centuries, people in the cities of Europe eagerly seized any chance to see a captive chimpanzee. Once Europeans learned that chimps are easy to train, the apes became entertainers, forced to do tricks. Their owners often dressed the chimps in human clothes and taught them to perform human actions, such as eating with spoons or riding ponies. Human audiences, it seemed, loved to watch apes mimicking them.

They still do. Chimpanzees are still part of modern entertainment. They roller-skate or ride on bicycles in circuses, movies,

IN 1699 ENGLISHMAN EDWARD TYSON WROTE THAT CHIMPANZEES HAD MANY CHARACTERISTICS SHARED BY HUMANS. SINCE THEN, SCIENTISTS HAVE ESTABLISHED THAT CHIMPS ARE OUR CLOSEST ANIMAL RELATIVES.

and television shows. Performing chimps often wear "cute" human costumes, such as little tuxedos or ballet tutus. Those outfits do more than highlight the chimps' appealing resemblance to people. They also hide the devices that trainers and owners use to control—and sometimes to punish—their performing animals. A performing chimp seen on television or at a live show may be tied down with a chain or cable that is kept out of view. A chimp that needs to move around freely during its act

Costumed chimpanzees dance to conga music as part of a circus show in Las Vegas in the 1970s. For centuries, people have used chimps as entertainers, often highlighting their resemblance to people by dressing them and training them to imitate human activities.

may wear an electrical device strapped to its body under its clothes. A trainer waits out of sight, his finger on a button, to give the ape a shock if it misbehaves. Performing chimps may also have some or all of their teeth removed or have their jaws fastened shut so that they cannot bite. Their faces may be shaved to give them a more human look.

Apes are most obedient and easiest to control when they are young, and the career of a performing chimp usually lasts only a few years. (Chimpanzee characters who perform over long periods of time, such as J. Fred Muggs early in the television era, or Zippy, the camera-wearing chimp often seen on David Letterman's late-night show, are played by many different animals in turn.) Sometimes the owners of performing chimps give the animals drugs to keep them calm, or treat them with hormones that make them more manageable by preventing their full physical or sexual development. No one knows what other effects these treatments might have on the apes.

Some mistreatment, sadly, is more brutal. Dale Peterson, a researcher who wrote about the relationship between chimpanzees and humans in the 1993 book *Visions of Caliban*, reports that some show-business apes are beaten by their owners or trainers as punishment for mistakes or for aggressive or violent behavior. But conditions are improving for performing chimpanzees. The American Zoo and Aquarium Association (AZA) has criticized the use of primates in entertainment, drawing closer attention to the treatment of performing chimps.

Fortunately, not all encounters between humans and chimpanzees are marked by exploitation or cruelty. Dedicated scientists in African forests and in primate-research labs around the world are studying chimpanzees. Many of these investigators feel respect, admiration, and affection for the animals they observe. They hope that their work will lead to better understanding of

J. Fred Muggs demonstrates a miniature pedal-powered Corvette at a 1956 auto show—he had trouble with the pedals, so he simply pushed the car along. The chimp known as Muggs was a popular entertainer for years, but the character was actually played by a series of animals.

chimpanzees—and also to greater protection from habitat loss, hunting, and human ignorance.

New Understanding

What fascinates people about chimpanzees, whether in zoos, circuses, or nature documentaries, is the way they blur the boundary between the human and animal worlds. Modern chimpanzee research has shown that chimpanzees and humans share many features of both biology and behavior.

By the end of the eighteenth century scientists had figured out that the chimpanzee and the orangutan are different animals. By the middle of the nineteenth they had described the gorilla, the largest ape, which, like the chimpanzee, is native to Africa. In 1929 they identified the bonobo, originally called the pygmy chimpanzee—the last known species of ape to be discovered. Identifying and describing the apes, however, was only the first step toward learning about them.

A new stage of primate research began in the 1920s and 1930s. By this time scientists had recognized monkeys and apes as humankind's closest biological relatives. They realized that these primates could play a useful role in medical research. Scientists could test medicines and surgeries on monkeys or apes before using them on humans. They could also examine apes' brains and nervous systems for clues about how those organs operate in humans. In addition, some scientists wanted to study primate behavior.

At first, researchers bought primates that had been captured in the wild. Soon, however, they established breeding stations to serve as reliable sources of animals. Russia set up one of the first primate research and breeding stations in 1927. Three years later, an American scientist named Robert Yerkes founded a similar station in Florida. It was later moved to Emory University in Georgia, where it still operates as the Yerkes Regional Primate Research Center, a leading center of primatology.

Science had recognized apes as physically or biologically related to humans, but most scientists felt that a great gulf separated humans from animals, even their closest kin. That gulf had to do with the nature of what it means to be human. The majority of experts believed that animals, including apes, simply could not do certain important things that define human beings. They could not use tools to manipulate their environments, for example, or use language. They could not plan, or pass new knowledge on from generation to generation, or create culture. They had brains, but they did not have minds.

During the 1960s, a series of startling announcements from two directions began to bridge the great gulf between humans and their nearest animal relatives. In Africa, a young Englishwoman, with no formal scientific training but with great interest in primates, had begun the first long-term study of wild chimpanzees at a place called the Gombe Stream Chimpanzee Reserve (now Gombe National Park in Tanzania). Her name was Jane Goodall, and within a few decades she had become a world-famous expert on chimpanzees. Goodall's discoveries, and those made by other researchers who followed her lead, have forever changed our view of how chimpanzees live. We now know that these apes do some things that were once

JANE GOODALL SHARES AN AFFECTIONATE MOMENT WITH A BABY CHIMPANZEE AT GOMBE NATIONAL PARK IN TANZANIA. A PIONEER IN MODERN CHIMPANZEE RESEARCH, GOODALL LEARNED ABOUT THE BEHAVIOR OF THESE ANIMALS BY BECOMING A MEMBER OF THEIR COMMUNITY.

thought to be human activities only, such as making tools and waging war.

While Goodall and other field researchers investigated chimpanzee society in its natural setting, another line of research unfolded in a handful of laboratories, mostly in the United States. It was led by psychologists, biologists, and anthropologists who wanted to learn how apes' minds work—and, in particular, whether apes could indeed be taught to "speak." Ape-language research has produced some impressive results, such as gorillas and chimpanzees who can communicate using sign language or computer keyboards. Although scientists do not agree on the significance of these results, ape-language studies have shown beyond doubt that primates have unexpected abilities. And in recent years a third line of research, the study of DNA, has shown that the genetic relationship between chimpanzees and humans is closer than the one between chimpanzees and orangutans or chimpanzees and gorillas. Humans are beginning to realize that the gulf between them and their nearest animal relatives is narrower than they once thought.

In 1971 Jane Goodall published a book about her early experiences studying wild chimpanzees at Gombe Stream. Called *In the Shadow of Man*, it introduced millions of readers to an extraordinary new view of primates. The book ends with the memory of a moment shared by Goodall and a chimpanzee she called David Graybeard, the first to accept her presence in the chimpanzee community. Her story reveals an understanding of chimpanzees that goes far beyond Battell's tale of a monster that could not speak:

One day, as I sat near [David] at the bank of a tiny trickle of crystal-clear water, I saw a ripe red palm nut lying on the ground. I picked it up and held it out to him on my open palm.

He turned his head away. When I moved my hand closer he looked at it, and then at me, and then he took the fruit, and at the same time held my hand firmly and gently with his own. As I sat motionless he released my hand, looked down at the nut, and dropped it to the ground.

At that moment there was no need of any scientific knowledge to understand his communication of reassurance. The soft pressure of his fingers spoke to me not through my intellect but through a more primitive emotional channel: the barrier of untold centuries which had grown up during the separate evolution of man and chimpanzee was, for those few seconds, broken down.

2 The Chimpanzee Family Tree

Jane Goodall wrote of "the separate evolution of man and chimpanzee" when she described her moment of understanding with David Graybeard. People and chimps have indeed evolved separately over the past few million years. However, humans and chimps, along with all other primates, are descended from the same ancestors. Since the early years of the twentieth century, one of science's most exciting missions has been mapping the complex path of primate evolution, from its beginnings in the distant past, beyond the dead ends and blind alleys that led to extinction, to the creatures alive today. The map is neither complete nor final, but scientists have learned some important things about the evolution of all primates, including humans. Along the way, our curiosity about our own origins paved the way for new discoveries about chimpanzees.

A FOSSIL JAW AND SKULL FOUND NEAR JOHANNESBURG, SOUTH AFRICA, ARE BETWEEN 1.5 AND 2 MILLION YEARS OLD. THEY ARE FROM *PARANTHROPUS ROBUSTUS*, A HOMINID THAT BECAME EXTINCT AROUND A MILLION YEARS AGO. NOT A DIRECT ANCESTOR OF MODERN HUMANS, *P. ROBUSTUS* WAS MORE LIKE A DISTANT COUSIN OF HUMAN ANCESTORS. THE JAWBONE IS FROM A MALE; THE SKULL, ONE OF THE MOST COMPLETE HOMINID SKULLS EVER FOUND, IS FROM A FEMALE.

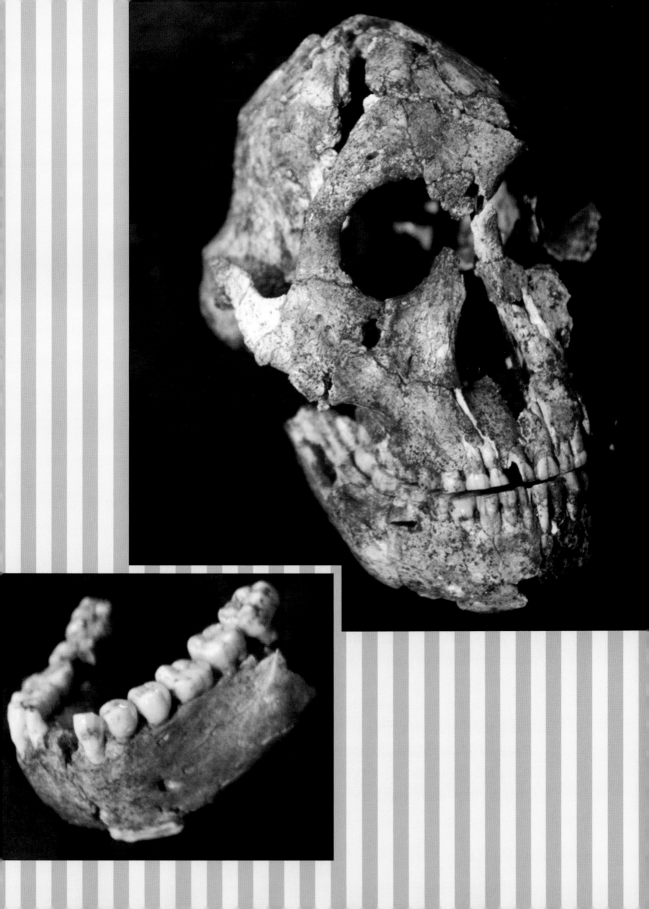

Primate Origins

Paleontology, the study of ancient and extinct life-forms, was founded on fossils. Much of what we know about evolution comes from studying the physical traces of past life. Paleontologists interested in primate evolution, though, face special challenges. Most of the primate species that have lived on Earth over many millions of years have been arboreal, or tree-dwelling, animals. Creatures that spend most of their time in forests are not the best candidates for fossilization. Fossils usually form after dead animals are covered by sand, mud, or ash. If this happens quickly, before other animals disturb or devour the body, the fossil may be fairly complete. Oceans, deserts, swamps, riverbanks, and volcanic plains all offer better chances for fossilization than the tropical forests where most primates have lived. For this reason scientists have found fewer fossils of primates than of many other groups of animals. Many primate fossils are simply small, single pieces, such as teeth.

The oldest known fossil that clearly belonged to a primate is a tooth found at Purgatory Hill in Montana. It comes from an extinct animal that scientists call *Purgatorius*. Experts think that this ancient primate was about as large as a mouse or rat. It may have looked much like some of the smaller modern prosimians, a group of primates that includes lemurs and galagos, or bush babies. The *Purgatorius* fossil dates from between 55 and 60 million years ago, leading paleontologists to believe that the primate group probably originated around that time, after the dinosaurs became extinct.

But a few researchers have challenged this traditional paleontological view of primate origins. In 2002 a team of experts at Chicago's Field Museum presented a new time scale for primate evolution based on statistical mathematics, not fossils. Using a formula that combined the number of living primate species, the number of extinct primate species known from fossils, and an estimated average "lifetime" of 2.5 million years for each species, the team produced a figure of 80 to 85 million years ago for primate origins. In other words, they think that the ancestor of all primates lived at that time—before the disappearance of the dinosaurs—even though no primate fossils have been found to support their claim. Only further investigation into the question of primate origins will settle the issue.

Whenever primates originated, the fossil record shows that they began evolving into new forms about 55 million years ago. Evolution gradually produced two primate groups known as the adapids and the omomyids. Their faces were flatter and less rodentlike than those of *Purgatorious* and its immediate descendants. Their brains and eyes were bigger. Instead of claws, they had flat nails on some of their toes. The first toe on each foot was set apart from the other toes and could curl in the opposite direction, a feature called an opposable thumb. All of these characteristics began to resemble those of modern primates.

Paleontologists do not know how the adapids and omomyids gave rise to the many groups of later primates. Many believe that adapids were the ancestors of lemurs and their close kin and omomyids were the ancestors of monkeys, apes, and small Asian primates called tarsiers. Others think that monkeys and apes may be descended from an unknown third group of early primates. Fossils recently uncovered in China and Egypt may shed light on where, when, and how anthropoids evolved.

Primates lived in many parts of the world until about 35 million years ago, when global temperatures cooled. A number of primates and other species vanished, probably because the lower temperatures brought changes in climate and vegetation. Still, many primate species remained, and they adapted to life under these new conditions. By 25 million years ago, ancestral apes called dryopithecines had evolved in Africa. In the ages that followed, many new species of prosimians, monkeys, and apes (also called anthropoids) evolved. Some became extinct and left no descendants in the modern world. Others gave rise to today's primates, including apes and humans. The evolution of apes and humans is a complex and controversial mystery in itself, one that began between 5 and 8 million years ago.

Apes and People

In 1859 English naturalist Charles Darwin launched the study of evolutionary biology with *On the Origin of Species*, the first book to describe evolution at length and to explain how it could have created the immense variety of plant and animal species. Darwin avoided a detailed discussion of human evolution, saying only, "Light will be thrown on the origin of man and his history." Still, it was clear that Darwin had opened the way to seeing human beings as products of evolution. It was also clear that human evolution must somehow be linked to that of anthropoids, because of the many features shared by people and apes.

One of Darwin's scientific supporters, Thomas Henry Huxley, wrote about human origins and evolution in 1863 in *Evidence for Man's Place in Nature*. Among other points, Huxley demonstrated that the physical structures of human, chimpanzee, and gorilla brains are very similar. In 1871 Darwin presented his own views on human evolution. In *The Descent of Man* he gathered the anatomical and fossil evidence for human kinship with other primates. Darwin did not think that humans evolved from any ape or monkey known in the modern world. Instead, he argued that humans and apes both evolved from the same long-extinct primate. At the early stages of evolution, he wrote, the ancestors of humans must have had some apelike qualities.

Ever since the publication of *On the Origin of Species*, some people have criticized or disagreed with the concept of evolution, largely because it conflicts with various religious beliefs. Even some who willingly accepted evolution as the source of plant and animal species had trouble accepting the fact that humans were also part of the animal world and its history. However, scientists recognized that evolution—including human evolution—was the best available explanation of observable facts about the natural world. Evolutionary biology became firmly established in scientific thought, although each year brings new discoveries, ideas, and sometimes disagreements about the details of evolution and the ways it operates.

From Darwin and Huxley to the twenty-first century, human evolution has aroused interest and curiosity. Today, those who investigate the subject have many fossils of early apes and humans to examine. Paleontologists are still working, however, to sort out the family history of hominoids and hominids. Hominoids are a subgroup of primates containing apes and humans and the extinct species that were their direct ancestors. Traditionally, scientists divided hominoids into three families. The lesser apes, the gibbons and siamangs of Asia, were the hylobatid family. The great apes—chimpanzees, gorillas, and orangutans—were the pongid family. Humans formed the hominid family. Included in the hominid family are several species of human ancestors, known from fossil remains to be humanlike creatures that walked upright on two legs. Some of them are the ancient hominids called australopithecines. The best-known australopithecine is probably "Lucy," a famous 3.5-million-year-old fossil found in East Africa in 1974. Other hominids are more recent species such as *Homo erectus*, the ancestor of modern humans (whose scientific classification is *Homo sapiens*).

If apes and humans are both hominoids, what ancestors did

Chimpanzees, like all primates, use facial expressions as a form of communication. In *The Expression of the Emotions in Man and Animals* (1872), Charles Darwin argued that humans and other animals, especially primates, share both facial expressions and the feelings that cause them. Earlier, Darwin had established the concept of evolution and demonstrated that humans and animals had evolved from shared ancestors.

they share and when did their evolutionary parts separate? The answer may lie in what paleontologists call the "hominoid gap"—a period between about 4 million and about 14 million years ago during which scientists noted a shortage of ape and hominid fossils from Africa. Scientists suspect that important changes occurred in primate evolution during those ten million years, but fossil evidence is scarce. By the end of the "gap," hominids existed, but little can be determined about early stages of their development.

At the time Lucy was discovered, many experts believed that the hominid line had split apart from the lines leading to the great apes about 20 million years ago. Since that time, however,

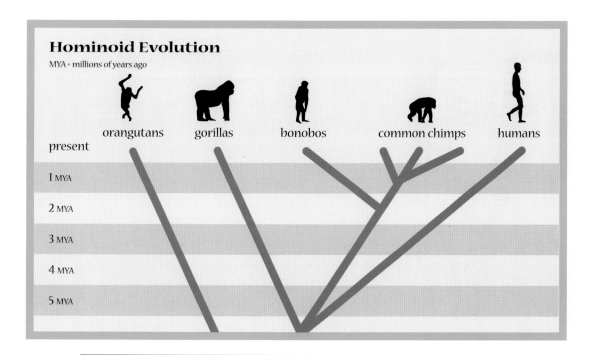

THOUGH EXPERTS ONCE BELIEVED THAT HUMANS BEGAN TO EVOLVE SEPARATELY FROM CHIMPS 20 MILLION YEARS AGO, THEY NOW THINK THE SPLIT OCCURRED ONLY 5 MILLION YEARS AGO.

new views of hominid evolution have emerged. In the 1980s scientists turned to biochemistry and genetics to find out how long various groups of modern primates had been evolving separately. By examining blood proteins, they could estimate the evolutionary "distance" between species. These studies suggested that human ancestors actually separated from the African apes only between 4 and 5 million years ago. Around the same time, researchers began analyzing the DNA of humans and apes, again hoping to find out how closely or distantly they are related. They were surprised to discover how close the relationship is.

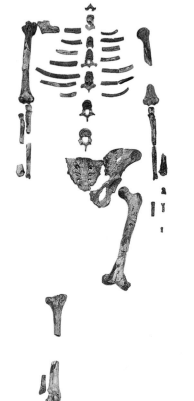

Most experts reported that humans and chimps share 98 to 99 percent of their genetic code (although a study released in 2002 by a biologist at the California Institute of Technology suggests that 95 percent may be more accurate). As a result of these studies, a new hominoid family tree has emerged. It shows the human and chimpanzee lines separating around 5 million years ago, although a few scientists have

IN 1974 PALEONTOLOGISTS WORKING IN ETHIOPIA UNEARTHED THE MOST COMPLETE FOSSIL SKELETON OF AN UPRIGHT-WALKING HUMAN ANCESTOR EVER FOUND. THE THREE-FOOT-TALL SKELETON IS CALLED LUCY BECAUSE THE RESEARCHERS PLAYED THE BEATLES SONG "LUCY IN THE SKY WITH DIAMONDS" AS THEY CELEBRATED THE FIND. AROUND 3.5 MILLION YEARS OLD, LUCY CAST NEW LIGHT ON WHAT HOMINIDS WERE LIKE SOON AFTER THE LINES LEADING TO HUMANS AND CHIMPANZEES SEPARATED.

argued that the split occurred as early as 8 million years ago or as recently as 3 million. Paleontologists continue to investigate the issue. Pinpointing the time of separation between apes and humans will help answer questions about how slowly or quickly human ancestors evolved into modern humans.

In addition to a new hominoid family tree, some scientists have called for changes in the way living hominid species are grouped into scientific families. Instead of using the traditional hylobatid, pongid, and hominid categories, some zoologists now place humans, chimpanzees, gorillas, and orangutans in a single category, although they do not agree on whether that category should be called pongids or hominids. Another approach is to group humans, chimpanzees, and gorillas together as hominids while leaving orangutans on their own in the pongid family. Just as paleontologists do not agree on a single family tree for primates, zoologists do not all agree on a single scheme of primate classification.

Research into human and chimpanzee evolution continues, driven by new laboratory techniques and new fossil finds. One such find was made in the North African country of Chad in 2002, when paleontologists found a skull thought to be 6 or 7 million years old. Some paleontologists, including those who found the skull, think that it is the oldest hominid fossil yet found, but other experts think it belonged to an ancient ape. Like other fossils and theories in the complicated field of primate evolution, the Chad skull is likely to spark debate for years to come.

The quest for information about human origins has produced much new knowledge—not all of it about human beings. An offshoot of research into hominid evolution led to a revolution in chimpanzee studies. In the late 1950s Jane Goodall was a young, eager assistant to Louis Leakey, a paleontologist working in East Africa. Leakey and members of his family later discovered

a number of important hominid fossils, but he set Goodall on a different path. He suggested that a study of chimpanzees living near Lake Tanganyika might show how early hominids could have lived and behaved in similar environments. Goodall "agreed wholeheartedly and enthusiastically to undertake the work," as she later recalled, and a year later she began her pioneering chimpanzee research at Gombe Stream.

Modern Chimpanzees

When Jane Goodall turned her attention from extinct hominids to living chimpanzees, she studied a population of animals known as eastern chimpanzees. Africa has two species and three known subspecies, or varieties, of chimpanzees in all. The two species are closely related and probably separated from each other about 2 million years ago. One is the common chimpanzee, and the other is the bonobo. Both belong to the genus *Pan*, a scientific classification within the order of primates. (Gorillas,

orangutans, and humans each belong to a genus of their own.)
Some scientists believe that the two species of chimpanzees may
interbreed in the wild on rare occasions. Several breedings have
occurred between captive common chimpanzees and bonobos.
The offspring are normal, fertile animals.

The common chimpanzee's scientific name is *Pan troglodytes*.
The range of this species extends across tropical Africa, from the

THREE JUVENILE ORANGUTANS IN BORNEO, SOUTHEAST ASIA. SOME OF THE FIRST
CHIMPANZEES IN EUROPE WERE THOUGHT TO BE ORANGUTANS, BUT SCIENTISTS SOON
REALIZED THAT CHIMPS AND ORANGS ARE SEPARATE SPECIES. LATER THEY DISCOVERED
THAT AFRICA IS HOME TO TWO SPECIES OF CHIMPANZEE.

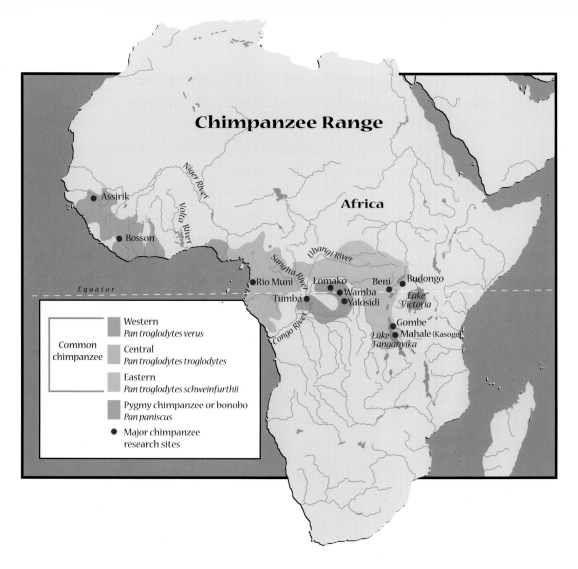

Chimpanzee Range

Africa

Common chimpanzee

Western
Pan troglodytes verus

Central
Pan troglodytes troglodytes

Eastern
Pan troglodytes schweinfurthii

Pygmy chimpanzee or bonobo
Pan paniscus

● Major chimpanzee research sites

vicinity of Lake Victoria in the east to the coast of Africa's great westward bulge. Most primatologists recognize three varieties, or subspecies, within the species. Each occupies a different part of the range. The eastern chimpanzee, *Pan troglodytes schweinfurthii*, is found in the countries of Tanzania, Rwanda, Burundi, Uganda, the Central African Republic, and the northern part of the Democratic Republic of Congo. The central chimpanzee, *Pan*, or *P. troglodytes troglodytes*, also lives in the Democratic Republic of Congo and in the nations of Congo, Gabon, Equatorial Guinea, Cameroon, and Nigeria. The western chimpanzee, *Pan*, or *P. troglodytes verus*, lives in the West African countries of Ivory Coast, Liberia, Guinea, Sierra Leone, Guinea-Bissau, Senegal, and Gambia. In all of these areas, chimpanzees' primary habitat is tropical forest, from lowlands to mountain heights of almost 10,000 feet (3,050 m). Chimps also live in dry, open grasslands, brushy scrub, and savanna. Since 2000, scientists have been investigating a little-known group of primates living in a region of the Democratic Republic of Congo. Skulls, photographs, DNA from hair samples, and other evidence suggest that these primates are most likely large common chimpanzees, although they have some of the features and behavior of gorillas. Scientists do not yet know whether the animals belong to one of the three known subspecies of common chimpanzee or should be considered a new, fourth subspecies.

The bonobo, *Pan paniscus*, has a much smaller range than the common chimpanzee. Bonobos occupy a small region in the Democratic Republic of the Congo, south of the Congo River, and live almost entirely in tropical forest. Little research was done on bonobos until the 1970s. Since that time primatologists have learned much about how bonobos compare with common chimpanzees in both appearance and behavior.

BONOBOS TEND TO HAVE DARKER SKIN AND HAIR, SMALLER AND FLATTER EARS, AND ROUNDER FOREHEADS THAN COMMON CHIMPANZEES.

3

Physical Features

Years ago, zoo animals were kept in small, barred cages, often with nothing to do and no contact with others of their kind. Many zoos, however, now take a more generous approach to housing captive animals. They create enclosures with plants, rocks, and trees that give the animals at least some qualities of life in natural surroundings. Perhaps no animals have benefited more from this trend than chimpanzees, who are active creatures. Captive chimps in today's zoos are usually given log structures or sets of ropes to climb. They are excellent climbers—evolution designed their bodies for life in the trees.

Two Species

Chimpanzees are no longer the mystery they were to Andrew Battell and his fellow Europeans in the seventeenth century. Modern primatologists have gathered a wealth of information

CHIMPANZEES' FACIAL SKIN, OFTEN PALE AT BIRTH, DARKENS IN PATCHES AS THE ANIMALS MATURE.

about all types of apes, including the most recently discovered species, the bonobo. For much of the twentieth century, scientists could not decide whether bonobos and common chimpanzees were really two separate species or whether bonobos were a subspecies of the common chimp. Now, however, the majority of primatologists consider them to be a separate species.

Common chimpanzees show a wide range of height at adulthood, measuring between 3.3 and 5.5 feet (100 and 170 cm) when standing. Males tend to be larger and more solidly built than females. Their average adult weight is 110 pounds (50 kg), compared with 90 pounds (41 kg) for females. Of the three subspecies, western and central chimpanzees are often a bit larger and heavier than eastern chimps. Captive chimpanzees of any subspecies are likely to be larger than average because they generally receive more food and engage in less physical activity than wild chimps.

As the name "pygmy chimpanzee" suggests, bonobos are generally smaller than common chimps, but the difference is not great. Although bonobos may be as tall as common chimpanzees, they are more slender, weighing between 75 and 100 pounds (34 and 45 kg). Male and female bonobos are closer in size than are common chimps.

Takayoshi Kano, a zoologist who directed Japanese research on bonobos, described some of the physical differences between the two species in his book, *The Last Ape*. He reported that the skin of bonobos is black throughout their lives, except for lighter pinkish or reddish-tan patches on their lips and around their eyes. Common chimps, in contrast, are born with pinkish-tan or light brown skin that usually freckles and then darkens as they grow older. Both species are typically born with black hair, although within each species a few individuals have brown or reddish-brown hair. Bonobos' hair remains black throughout their lives, while common chimpanzees' hair may turn light brown or even gray when they become adults. Common chimpanzees also are likely to become bald on their foreheads as they age, but bonobos rarely become bald (except in captivity—zoo chimpanzees of both species and both sexes frequently show some baldness). In addition, bonobos' heads are slightly smaller for their size than those of common chimps, and they are rounder. Bonobos' foreheads are higher and more rounded than those of common chimps. The ridges of bone above their eyes are less pronounced, and their ears are smaller and lie flatter against the sides of their heads.

Anatomy

In spite of their differences, bonobos and common chimpanzees are very similar in their basic anatomy. Some of their anatomical features are shared by all primates, while others are found only in hominoids, the subgroup of primates that includes apes and humans.

Primate anatomy is clearly visible in the skull, which has a large central cavity to house the brain. Primates' braincases are larger, in proportion to their overall body size, than those of other similar-size animals, and chimpanzees have the biggest brains of any primates other than humans. Modern studies of ape and human brains show that Thomas Henry Huxley was right when he claimed that there are no structural differences between them. The main difference is size. The brain of an average adult bonobo or common chimpanzee weighs about 14.4 ounces (410 g), less than a pound. Human brain weight varies over a wide range, from 35 to 63 ounces (1,000 g to 1,800 g), but is always significantly higher than that of the largest ape. There may be other differences that are not visible. Scientists who

Chimpanzee Skull

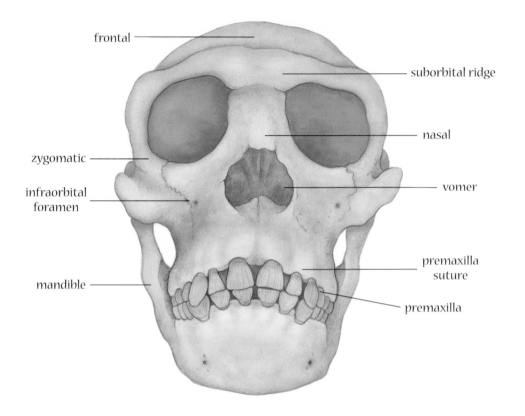

frontal

suborbital ridge

nasal

zygomatic

vomer

infraorbital
foramen

premaxilla
suture

mandible

premaxilla

study brain function think that even species with very similar brains may use their brains' "wiring" in different ways—ways that are not yet fully understood.

Chimpanzee skulls have large orbits—the cavities that hold the eyeballs. The large size of chimpanzees' eyes shows that they make considerable use of their sense of sight. The position of the orbits shows that a chimp's eyes face forward, not out to the sides like those of many other animals. This placement allows the fields of vision of the chimp's two eyes to overlap a great deal. Binocular or stereoscopic vision, as this kind of vision is called, gives its owner good depth perception, the ability to judge how far away things are. For a creature that spends time in the treetops, jumping or swinging from branch to branch, such an ability may be a lifesaver.

An animal's teeth are a clue to the kinds of food it is adapted to eat. Chimpanzees and humans both have thirty-two teeth, although the incisors or canine teeth, the four long, sharp teeth at the front corners of the mouth, are longer and stronger in chimpanzees. The two incisors in the chimp's bottom jaw are wedge-shaped, with wide, sharp upper surfaces. They are ideal for biting through tough materials such as fruit rinds or nutshells. The upper incisors are longer and more pointed than the lower ones. They are used in fighting and are larger in males than in females. Behind the incisors, along the sides of the jaw, are upper and lower rows of flat teeth called premolars and molars: the chewing teeth. The rear molars are sturdy, with uneven upper surfaces to crush and grind tough plants. Like humans, chimpanzees have all-purpose teeth—not as good as a cow's teeth for grinding grass or as good as a tiger's for slashing flesh, but useful for eating a diet of both plant and animal foods. Both species are omnivores, meaning that they eat all kinds of foods. Chimpanzees' diets, however, contain considerably more plant material than meat.

Most mammals, including chimpanzees, share the same basic body structure. A mammal's body is something like a table: a body carried horizontally and supported by four limbs, two in front and two in back. However, the limbs evolved somewhat differently in various groups of mammals. Animals who spent all of their time on the ground, such as pigs and horses, developed four legs of more or less equal length, each ending in the same kind of foot. But animals who lived at least part of the time in the trees, such as monkeys and apes, developed forelimbs and hind limbs suited to different purposes. Their forelimbs, or arms,

Chimpanzee Skeleton

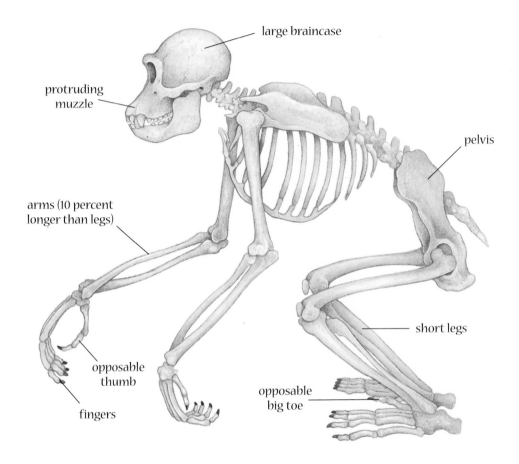

large braincase

protruding
muzzle

pelvis

arms (10 percent
longer than legs)

short legs

opposable
thumb

opposable
big toe

fingers

rotate in all directions from their shoulder joints. This allows chimps to reach overhead and out to either side when climbing—motions impossible for a deer or a dog. Chimps can also fold their arms across their own bodies to cradle or carry things. The chimpanzee's hind limbs, or legs, have thicker bones and support more of the animal's weight. The hip joints do not have the same mobility as the shoulder joints, but they are more stable. Although chimpanzees are built a lot like human beings, and many of them are smaller than people, the average adult chimpanzee is much stronger than the average human being. Compared with people, chimpanzees have broad shoulders and big arms for their size. They are also more muscular and are about four times as strong as humans.

Chimpanzees' hands are also larger and stronger, relative to body size, than those of humans. The animals' hands look very much like their feet. During the nineteenth century, scientists classified chimpanzees and other apes as quadrumana, which meant "four-handed creatures." The term fell out of use, and today scientists refer to chimps as having both hands and feet. They know, however, that these parts of a chimpanzee's body are more versatile than those of humans. Chimpanzees can use their hands for walking and their feet for picking things up or grasping. A chimp's fingers bend and curl just like a human's, and so can its toes, unlike human toes. Like a human, a chimp has an

Chimpanzee Hand and Foot

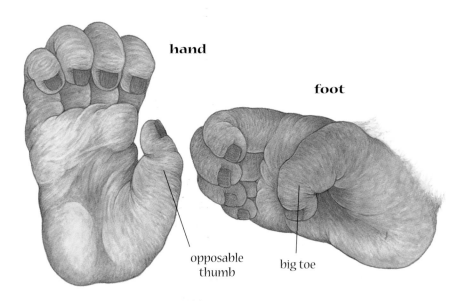

hand

foot

opposable thumb

big toe

opposable pollex, or thumb, that can curl toward the fingertips for precise gripping and holding. Unlike a human, however, a chimp also has a hallux, or big toe, that is set apart from the other toes at the side of the foot. It looks and operates like a thumb, with a grip strong enough to support the animal's weight. The tips of chimpanzees' fingers and toes may be as sensitive as human fingertips. They have dense networks of nerves that sense pressure, temperature, and texture. Broad, flat nails, similar to those on human digits, protect the ends of the chimpanzees' fingers and toes. Strong, delicate, and flexible, chimpanzee hands and feet can handle things almost as well as human hands and are better adapted to climbing and hanging.

Hominids are bipedal, meaning that they walk upright on two feet all of the time. Humans are the only hominids in the world today. Our hominoid relatives, chimpanzees and the other apes, can walk upright on two feet, but they don't do so all of the time. Mostly, chimpanzees move about using both their arms and their legs. They are adapted to movement in trees and on the ground—or, as scientists say, to both arboreal and terrestrial locomotion.

In trees, chimpanzees climb using both arms and legs. They can cling to trunks or branches with any or all of their limbs. They can also swing by their arms from branch to branch. Zoologists use the term "modified brachiation" or "semi-brachiation" to describe the arm-swinging of chimpanzees. Brachiation is the way that gibbons and siamangs, the lesser apes, swing from branch to branch using first one hand and then the other. With each new swing and handgrip, they rotate their bodies so that they are facing to one side or another, and they can travel very fast in this way. Orangutans and chimps are modified brachiators. They swing from branch to branch, hanging from their hands, but they do not twist their bodies with each swing like the lesser

With big toes that are as flexible and opposable as its thumbs, a chimpanzee can hang and move about in trees as though it has four hands. Scientists used to call apes quadrumana, or "four-handed creatures."

Both species of chimpanzees can and sometimes do walk bipedally, or upright on two feet, as this bonobo is doing.

THE MISTS OF EARLY MORNING SWIRL THROUGH AN EQUATORIAL AFRICAN FOREST AS A CHIMPANZEE LEAPS FROM TREE TO TREE. ALTHOUGH CHIMPS ARE CAPABLE OF DARING LEAPS, THEY ALSO TRAVEL BETWEEN TREES BY WALKING ON THE GROUND.

apes. They face forward as they swing, and unlike the lesser apes, often pause between swings. Many observers have reported that bonobos are more acrobatic in trees than common chimpanzees, perhaps because they are more slender. Their narrower shoulders let them pass more easily between branches. Bonobos make bolder jumps from tree to tree than chimpanzees do, and they are also more likely to dive between branches or trees in a head-down position.

On the ground, both species of chimpanzees usually move quadrupedally, which means they walk on all fours. With the soles of their feet flat on the ground, they walk on the knuckles of their hands, with the fingers folded under and pointing back toward the body. Their weight rests mostly on the knuckles of their second and third fingers. Knuckle-walking reveals another anatomical difference between common chimpanzees and bonobos. The arms of common chimps are significantly longer than their legs. When chimps knuckle-walk or stand on all fours, their backs are slanted, with shoulders much higher than hips. Bonobos' arms and legs, however, are closer to the same length. When bonobos are on all fours, their backs are less slanted. All chimpanzees can stand and walk upright, but they generally only do so for short periods or under special circumstances—for example, when they are using their hands to carry things, or when they want to see as far as possible. When chimpanzees walk standing up, each step is flat-footed—the entire foot touches the ground at once. Humans, in contrast, use a striding gait, hitting the ground first with their heels and pushing off from each step with their toes.

Chimpanzees' internal organs and systems are quite a bit like those of humans. The chimpanzee even has an appendix, a sac or pouch that is part of the digestive system but has no purpose in digestion. Humans are all too familiar with this anatomical

Chimpanzee Organs

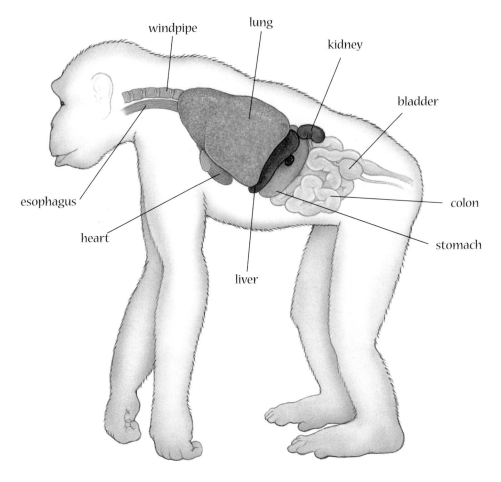

nuisance, which can cause illness and even death if it becomes inflamed or infected. When this happens to a person, a surgeon removes the appendix; some captive chimpanzees have had the same operation. The appendix is present in all apes and some monkeys but does not occur in any other animals. It is a relic of a stage in primate evolution before monkeys, apes, and humans split into different lines of descent.

A Chimp's View of the World

The senses of sight, hearing, smell, taste, and touch are sometimes called the special senses because each is connected to a special nerve center in the brain. By determining which nerve centers are largest and most developed, scientists can discover which senses are most important to an animal. In this way they have learned about primate senses in general and about how chimpanzees, in particular, sense the world.

Primates rely much more on sight and much less on smell than any other mammal group. The parts of their brains that process visual signals are large and complex, while the parts that process olfactory signals, or odors, are smaller than in other kinds of animals. Most primates find food by looking for it rather than by listening or sniffing—this is because the majority of primates eat mostly plant foods such as fruits and nuts, which make no noise and are often odorless.

Chimpanzees have very good eyesight. Their binocular vision gives them good depth perception, and they also have color vision (which may have adapted to help them identify

CHIMPANZEES VIEW THE WORLD VERY MUCH AS HUMANS DO—PERHAPS EMOTIONALLY, AND DEFINITELY VISUALLY. RESEARCHERS BELIEVE THAT THEIR SENSE OF SIGHT AND COLOR AND DEPTH PERCEPTION IS THE SAME AS OURS.

ripe fruits). Chimps, in fact, probably see the world much as human beings do. Their sense of hearing is also very similar to that of humans. Chimpanzees have sharper olfactory senses than humans, though. The olfactory nerve centers in their brains are slightly more developed, and the membranes in their noses have more olfactory cells to pick up scent molecules in the air during breathing. But the difference between chimps' and humans' senses of smell is not large. Both perform poorly compared with animals such as dogs and cats, who communicate through scent.

Where taste is concerned, chimpanzees and humans have the same kinds of taste buds on their tongues for sensing sweet, sour, salty, and bitter tastes. In their natural habitats chimpanzees

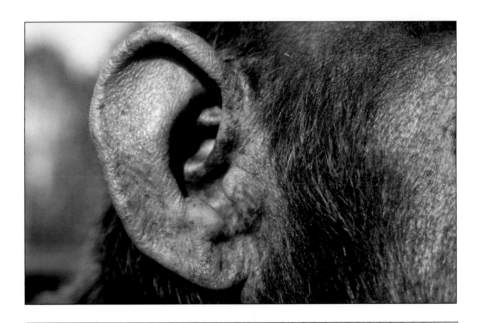

A CHIMPANZEE'S EAR IS VERY SIMILAR TO THAT OF A HUMAN BEING, AND SO IS ITS SENSE OF HEARING. MANY CAPTIVE CHIMPS SEEM TO ENJOY MUSIC, AND SOME EVEN APPEAR TO HAVE FAVORITE KINDS OF MUSIC AND FAVORITE SINGERS.

consume foods with a wide range of tastes. Captive chimps sometimes show preferences for certain kinds of snacks, such as salty chips or sweet candy. Their fondness for things that are not very good for them makes chimps seem very human. In her book *In My Family Tree*, which describes her experiences caring for orphaned, abandoned, and homeless chimps, Sheila Siddle tells of a chimp named Ludmilla, rescued by Jane Goodall from a hotel in Tanzania where she had spent years as a novelty attraction in the bar. During her time in the saloon Ludmilla had developed a fondness for Coca-Cola, beer, tea, and even cigarettes.

4 Life Cycle

Under ideal conditions, a wild chimpanzee may reach an age of fifty-three years, and captive ones often live even longer. During life spans longer than those of some people, chimpanzees pass through infancy, adolescence, maturity, and old age, just as people do. In each stage they are part of a chimpanzee community, a band or tribe that can provide both comfort and conflict. As Jane Goodall charted the development and interactions of chimps at Gombe Stream, she wrote,

> *Eventually the detailed understanding of chimpanzee behavior that will result from our long-term research at the Gombe will help man in his attempts to understand more of himself. . . . Yet it is not only for this reason that we continue our work year in, year out; we are also fascinated by the chimpanzees as individual beings. We want to know how Fifi, whom we first knew as a small infant, will look after her own children;*

CHIMPANZEE GROUPS OFTEN CONSIST OF A MOTHER AND SEVERAL YOUNG OF VARIOUS AGES. OLDER OFFSPRING APPEAR AFFECTIONATE TOWARD YOUNGER ONES, OFTEN CARRYING, GROOMING, AND PLAYING WITH THEM.

whether Flo survives to be a grandmother, and if so how she will react to Fifi's infant; what happens to Flint when his mother finally dies; whether Figan one day may become the top-ranking male.

As researchers collected such observations over many years, a richly detailed picture of the chimpanzee's life history emerged.

Birth and Infancy

Zoologists have found that, in general, animals with larger brains give birth to young that require longer periods of care. They also give birth to fewer young at a time. Chimpanzee mothers almost always bear single infants, although twins are born on rare occasions. A pregnant female chimp's gestation period, during which the unborn infant develops inside her, is usually 220 to 230 days for bonobos and 230 to 245 days for common chimpanzees. Pregnancy is less noticeable in chimpanzees than in humans. Caretakers of captive or rescued chimpanzees have reported that even when they see chimps daily they do not always realize that a female has become pregnant until she is close to giving birth or even appears before them with a new baby. Most captive chimps are tested to see if they are pregnant so that caretakers can be prepared for an expected birth.

Among wild chimpanzees, birth usually takes place in a tree nest—a platform or basket of bent branches supported by the fork of a tree. If no suitable site for a tree nest is available, a chimpanzee will make a leafy nest in shrubs or in any quiet, private place. Birth usually occurs more quickly for chimps than for human mothers. A baby chimp's head is smaller in relation to the mother's pelvis than that of a human infant, so the infant

chimp passes through the birth canal somewhat more easily. Newborn chimps are fairly small, with an average birth weight of just under 4 pounds (1.9 kg).

Infant chimpanzees are entirely helpless and cannot survive without food and protection. Like all newborn mammals, a baby chimpanzee is nourished with milk from its mother's mammary glands. A chimpanzee mother suckles its young just as a human mother does, holding the infant to its chest and guiding the baby's mouth to its nipple. A baby chimp suckles for several minutes every hour. In a few known cases, when females with infants have died or been killed, other female chimpanzees who were nursing their own young have adopted and suckled the orphans—an act that zoologists call allomothering. More commonly, however, the death of a mother chimpanzee also spells death for its infant. A chimpanzee baby's father is no more interested than any other adult male in the community in an infant or its welfare. Jane Goodall, however, documented a case in which a young adult male called Spindle adopted an orphaned infant named Mel. At just over three years old, Mel could survive without breast milk, but he needed protection. Spindle carried Mel, shared his sleeping nest with the young chimp, and kept him out of harm's way. Wrote Goodall, "Spindle saved Mel's life." Even after it no longer needs its mother's milk, a very young chimpanzee is neither strong nor experienced enough to face life on its own.

Field researchers have learned that a mother's first appearance with a new baby can be a time of excitement, even tension, in a chimpanzee community. The other chimps crowd around, curious and eager to see the infant. If the mother is young and inexperienced, she may show signs of fear or anger and may prevent the other chimps from getting close. This, in turn, may irritate the other adults, especially the males, and the mother may be forced to run from them with her newborn and wait until things quiet down a bit before returning. Older, more experienced females generally remain quiet and allow others in their community to look at the new baby, but they do not let adult males get close enough to touch a newborn. Mother chimps may allow other females, especially their own mothers or other relatives, to touch and handle their young, but usually not during the first few days of the baby's life.

Those first few days can be dangerous. Newborn chimps cannot grip tightly to their mothers' hair and must be held at all times. Mothers usually cradle their newborns in one hand, using the other to walk or run. In case of a fight or attack, a mother who is running or climbing for her life may lose her grip on her infant. Male chimpanzees can be dangerous to infants as well. Males often engage in charging displays, which are shows of aggressive behavior meant to establish dominance over others. A charging male makes lots of noise and dashes forward furiously. Most of

A BONOBO MOTHER CRADLES HER INFANT WHILE SHE FEEDS. ALTHOUGH THIS
ANIMAL IS STRIPPING LEAVES FROM A TWIG, A TYPICAL BONOBO'S DIET CONSISTS
MOSTLY OF FRUIT.

A FEMALE CHIMPANZEE PROTECTIVELY CLASPS HER INFANT. INFANTS STAY CLOSE TO
THEIR MOTHERS UNTIL THEY LEARN THE WAYS OF THE WORLD.

the time, someone backs down or retreats before the display
leads to actual fighting. Charging males, however, seem to
become caught up in the violent emotions of the moment, and
sometimes they have been known to grab infants who cross
their paths, dragging or shaking them.

Occasionally, adult chimpanzees of both sexes deliberately
attack and kill infants, sometimes devouring them. Most of these
cases have involved infants born to mothers who were newcomers to the group. Infanticide, as the killing of the young is
called, shocked and distressed the observers who first witnessed
it. However, its evolutionary purpose is clear. Infanticide eliminates
the possibility that the group will spend energy and resources

raising a young chimp that may have been fathered by a male outside the group. The infant's death also makes the female available for mating sooner than she would if she were raising her young. Males from the group will mate with her to ensure that her next infant will be one of their own.

No one is certain how often infanticide occurs among wild chimpanzees, but some researchers think that it is rarer among bonobos than common chimpanzees because female bonobos do not move from group to group as often as female common chimps do. Keeping her infant out of harm's way is one of a mother chimp's most important responsibilities. Once the group has accepted an infant's presence, however, the adults generally treat it with gentleness, or at least tolerance.

A YOUNG CHIMPANZEE VIEWS THE WORLD FROM ITS MOTHER'S BACK. CHIMPS AS OLD AS FIVE OR SIX YEARS MAY SEEK THE SECURITY OF THIS FAMILIAR PERCH WHEN THEY ARE FRIGHTENED OR NERVOUS.

Within a few hours or days of birth, a baby chimpanzee develops several important physical abilities. Its eyes begin to focus, so it can make out things around it. It begins flexing its fingers and toes into tight grips so it can cling to its mother's hair. She carries the infant under her body as she moves about on all fours, and although the baby holds on to her belly fur, she often gives it additional support with one hand. She holds the baby close to her as she sleeps.

Starting in the infant chimp's third or fourth month, it takes new steps—literally. It begins to stand, holding on to its mother. During its fifth month it begins walking on its own, first on all fours and later bipedally, and it starts climbing up tree branches in front of its mother. Like a human baby, the infant chimp is clumsy and uncertain at first, but it learns quickly. Its mother does not let it wander far. She continues to carry it most of the time, and from the fifth month on it sometimes rides on her back rather than under her belly. This new arrangement lets the mother move more freely and quickly, and it also gives the young chimp a wider view of the world.

Sometime during the third month the infant begins to sample solid food, tasting bits of whatever its mother is eating. It continues to suckle from its mother, however, even as it begins to consume greater amounts of solid food. Chimpanzees do not pass from infancy to maturity quickly or in a single step. Their helpless babyhood leads to a long period of learning and growing, all under the supervision of their mothers.

Growing Up

Primatologists divide chimpanzees' life history into stages. Infancy lasts for the first five years of life. During this time the young chimps need care, protection, and training from adult chimps. It

A MOTHER CHIMPANZEE WITH HER
YOUNG. INFANTS START STANDING
AND WALKING ON THEIR OWN
BETWEEN THE THIRD AND FIFTH
MONTHS OF LIFE, BUT THEY REMAIN
CLOSE TO THEIR MOTHERS, WHO
CARRY THEM FROM PLACE TO PLACE.

DURING THE DAY,
CHIMPANZEES OFTEN
REST OR NAP IN
TREES. THEY SIT IN
THE FORKS OF
BRANCHES AND SOME-
TIMES MAKE SMALL
NESTS OF BRANCHES
AND LEAVES.

is rare for chimps under five years old to survive without such protection. The next stage is the juvenile period, from five to eight years of age. During this period the young chimpanzee remains close to its mother, although she has most likely given birth to another infant by this time. The next stage of life is subadulthood or adolescence, during which chimpanzees generally become increasingly independent, although they may still have close ties with their mothers and siblings. These early phases of life introduce young chimps to two vital sets of skills. Survival skills are the knowledge and experience the chimps will need to survive in the physical world: how to find food, make nests, avoid predators, and generally take care of themselves. Social skills prepare the young for a lifetime of interacting and communicating with other chimpanzees.

As a chimp progresses through infancy, it is able to eat more and more solid food. Its mother usually weans it, or stops letting it suckle, when it is about four years old. By this time the young chimpanzee can move and climb quite well, but mothers often continue to carry three- and four-year-old infants, at least part of the time. Even older youngsters may run to their mothers and leap onto their backs to be carried when they are frightened, confused, tired, or simply eager for closeness.

Young chimps are intensely and endlessly curious about the world around them. They quickly learn to use their nimble hands to explore that world. Infant and juvenile chimpanzees spend a lot of time touching and handling things. Mother and baby chimps exchange many affectionate touches, from kisses to strokes, pats, and tickles (which most chimpanzees love). Infant chimps also touch other members of the community. Mothers allow infants to touch older siblings or friendly females but generally try to keep them from contact with males, at least until they are a few years old. They encourage their young, however, to touch and

CHIMPANZEES ARE COMMUNAL ANIMALS, WITH A NEED FOR AFFECTION AND CONTACT WITH OTHERS. IT IS NOT UNCOMMON FOR TWO ANIMALS TO FORM A LIFELONG FRIENDSHIP.

handle objects. At first a young chimp simply examines whatever its mother gives it, usually pieces of food but sometimes also leaves, twigs, stones, or—in the case of captive chimps—toys. Gradually the youngster begins copying its mother, learning to peel fruit and crack nutshells. As with walking, it begins clumsily but soon develops control. Before long the young chimpanzee is watching its mother find food and copying her actions.

Infant and juvenile chimps copy other kinds of behavior as well. Goodall observed Flint at ten months of age trying to make nests on the ground by bending twigs and grass stems. Soon he was experimenting with twigs in trees, too. After their first birthdays, most chimps are able to make small tree nests. By the end of the infant stage they can make their own full-size nests, and they are ready to begin sleeping on their own when their mothers have new infants. Young chimpanzees also copy the sexual activities of adults. They are very interested in sexual behavior and gather to watch matings. Afterward they often imitate the movements of mating adults. Primatologists are not certain what purpose this sexual play serves. It may simply be practice for the encounters the chimps will have after they reach sexual maturity,

A YOUNG CHIMPANZEE IN DISTRESS CALLS FROM A TREETOP IN A SANCTUARY IN ZAIRE, AFRICA.

or it may encourage glands in the young chimps' bodies to release chemicals that move them toward maturity.

Play of all kinds is a big part of chimpanzee childhood. Healthy young chimps, like healthy human children, seem at times to be bursting with energy. If a young chimp is with its mother or a group of adults, without playmates its own age, it will amuse itself by jumping, running, swinging from or bouncing on branches, and rolling about on the ground. But all young chimps love to play with other youngsters. They wrestle and engage in wild chases through the trees and across the ground. These activities not only improve their physical strength and

YOUNG CHIMPANZEES SPEND CONSIDERABLE TIME PLAYING WITH EACH OTHER. THROUGH PLAY, THEY FORM A HIERARCHY, OR "PECKING ORDER," THAT SHAPES THEIR SOCIAL INTERACTIONS THROUGHOUT LIFE.

coordination but also teach the young chimps necessary survival and social skills, as Goodall and others have noted. While playing in trees, young chimps often make bigger and bolder leaps than they would normally make when simply moving from place to place to eat. These daring leaps and drops give them experiences they can draw on later in life if they are involved in a fight in the treetops. Through wrestling and play-fighting, young chimps match their strength against each other. Their encounters, which may include biting and hitting, rarely result in real injuries.

Physical strength is not the only quality measured in the play of young chimps. By acting out adult behavior such as charging displays, individuals learn social skills and test their ability to dominate each other. Some youngsters refuse to back down in the face of such bluster and may respond with more vigorous displays. These individuals will probably become dominant members of the community when they are older. Others like to avoid confrontation. They quickly submit, or give in, to the more forceful youngsters. In this way young chimps form a hierarchy, or "pecking order," among themselves that will influence their future interactions. They are not without supervision as they do so, however. Mothers, older sisters, and even grandmothers watch the youngsters. These adult females have a pecking order, too, and a dominant or high-ranking mother may chase or snap at the offspring of a lower-ranking mother if play gets out of hand. Lower-ranking females, though, rarely discipline the young of higher-ranking females—such behavior might bring on an attack from the dominant mother. The play of young chimps is intertwined in the complex web of social rankings and relationships that makes up chimpanzee society.

In order to function as a member of that society, a growing chimp must learn to communicate. Chimps communicate through body language and gestures, facial expressions, and sounds. Posture is the most important kind of body language. It is used to establish relations between dominant and submissive or subordinate animals. A dominant or aggressive chimp stands tall, hair bristling, often waving its arms or beating the ground with sticks.

BONOBOS AND CHIMPANZEES COMMUNICATE THROUGH A WIDE RANGE OF FACIAL EXPRESSIONS, GESTURES, AND SOUNDS.

A submissive chimp crouches or squats, perhaps with its back to the dominant animal. Chimpanzees often greet one another by touching or even shaking hands. The more submissive animal reaches out first toward the dominant one, who reassures him or her with a gentle touch. Chimps of all ranks also show companionship through hand-holding, hugs, and smacking kisses.

Chimpanzees can display a wide variety of expressions, thanks to their mobile lips. A wide grin is a sign of fear, nervousness, or hostility, especially if the upper teeth and gums are showing. Such a grin may signal aggressive behavior. Aggressive chimpanzees also sometimes press their lips tightly together. An open-mouthed expression with the upper teeth covered, the jaw dropped, and the lower teeth exposed is a playful or excited expression, something like a human grin or laugh. Facial expressions play a large part in face-to-face communication, but chimpanzees also communicate with sound. That is the only way they can communicate over distances.

Researchers at Gombe have documented more than thirty different chimp vocalizations, each with its own meaning. Chimps scream to signal danger or anger, howl or wail when they are afraid or in pain, bark to announce the discovery of food, chuckle or laugh when amused, and grunt quietly while peacefully grooming or eating. Infants and mothers communicate with whimpers, clucks, and soft hoo-hoo sounds. Common chimpanzees frequently make a sound that Goodall calls a pant-hoot: a string of hoots with fast, heavy breaths between each sound. Pant-hoots serve as greetings among groups and individuals—every chimp has its own distinct pant-hoot, which others recognize. Members of groups keep in touch by pant-hooting as they move through trees or grass. Bonobos' pant-hoots are slightly different and higher-pitched. Listeners describe them as a series of hi-hi-hi sounds.

Adulthood

After several years as adolescents, or subadults, most chimpanzees reach their full size and are quite capable of living on their own. They are considered adults after they reach sexual maturity, the age at which they can father or bear young. Females typically become sexually mature in their eleventh year, males in their thirteenth. However, females generally do not bear their first young until they are fourteen or fifteen. They may continue having infants into their forties, although sometimes by that age they have become less fertile, which means that although they mate they do not easily become pregnant.

Throughout their reproductive lives, females usually mate, become pregnant, and give birth every five years or so, unless an infant dies—a female who loses her offspring will probably become pregnant again soon. Typically, an adult female chimpanzee "mothers" an infant and a juvenile who remain close to her or under her supervision. In addition, an older adolescent may still be part of the family. Female juveniles and adolescents often play with, groom, or care for their infant siblings.

As chimpanzees grow older, they show some of the signs of aging that we see in human beings. Their skin becomes wrinkled and saggy, and they may become stiff and slow in their movements. Their hair turns gray or white, especially on the face, head, and chest, and they may become partially bald. Chimpanzees suffer from many of the same illnesses that trouble humans, such as colds, pneumonia, epilepsy, cancer, arthritis, and polio. Chimps can also be troubled by parasites such as fleas, intestinal worms, and microscopic organisms that carry disease. Field researchers must take great care not to introduce diseases to chimpanzees or to catch illnesses or parasites from them.

An elderly chimp's status depends upon its gender. Females

An adult female chimpanzee. Like humans, chimps often acquire gray hairs with advancing age.

tend to keep their dominant ranking among the other females throughout their lives. Males, however, drop down the dominance rankings as they grow older. They are replaced by younger, stronger males at the top of the hierarchy. Even so, in most cases older males are treated with courtesy. Some younger animals may share food with them, wait for them when they move slowly, or show affection for them through such behavior as grooming and patting. When a chimpanzee dies, old or young, members of its family or group may show signs of distress, lingering by the body and stroking it. Takayoshi Kano reports in *The Last Ape* that when one female infant bonobo died, her adolescent male brother—who had always shown fondness for his little sister by carrying, tickling, and playing with her—carried her lifeless body around for a day and, when night fell, placed it carefully in the fork of a tree near his own nest.

5 Behavior

When modern chimpanzee field research began at Gombe Stream in 1960, it started as an effort to learn more about human beings by studying their closest relatives. But chimpanzees quickly became an absorbing subject of study in their own right. Studies of chimpanzee behavior have produced many surprising discoveries, from complex and sometimes startling features of chimp society to the animals' astonishing use of tools and language. But many of those who have spent years observing chimps, whether in the wild or in captivity, cannot avoid comparing them to people. As Sheila Siddle, creator of a chimpanzee sanctuary in Zambia, writes, "We really aren't that far apart." Behavior, even more than biology, reveals just how similar—and how different—chimpanzees and humans are.

CHIMPANZEES EATING TOGETHER. MOST CHIMPANZEES AND BONOBOS SPEND THEIR TIME IN SMALL GROUPS CALLED PARTIES, MOVING THROUGH THEIR HOME RANGE, FEEDING, AND NAPPING.

Social Structures

Field research has revealed many details of chimpanzees' social organizations and mating patterns. These aspects of life differ in some ways for common chimpanzees and bonobos.

Both species of chimps form large groups called communities. The members of a community do not all live together, and they may never all gather in the same place. They do, however, recognize one another by sight, sound, or smell. They share a tract of land called a home range or territory. Members of the community move about within that range and defend it against outsiders. The number of chimps in a community and the typical size of their territory varies according to species and environment.

Common chimpanzees' communities number between fifteen and eighty individuals; the average number is around fifty. In forests and woodlands, where trees are numerous and food resources such as fruit and nuts are concentrated, a community's territory may be as small as 2 square miles (5 km²) or as large as 15.5 square miles (40 km²). Territories average about 4.6 square miles (12 km²). But in savanna, where food is spread more thinly across the landscape, territories are larger. Researchers have estimated savanna territories at 46 to 216 square miles (120 to 560 km²), although they have also reported some chimp communities living in much smaller savanna territories.

On average, bonobo communities are slightly larger than those of common chimps, and so are their territories. Communities range from 40 to 120 individuals, territories from 8.5 to 25.3 square miles (22 to 65.5 km²). All bonobo territories are located in lowland forest, the species' only habitat.

Within communities, chimps of both species spend most of their time in smaller groups called parties. These are loose and flexible associations whose membership changes frequently. In the course of a day, or even an hour, a chimpanzee may be part of several different parties. Bonds between particular individuals, however, may remain stable over long periods, even over lifetimes, and these chimps can form the core of their own evershifting party. Brothers, in particular, tend to stay together over time.

A typical party of common chimpanzees consists simply of a female and her offspring. A larger party could include several females, their offspring and grandchildren, and perhaps one or two adult males. Adult males also join together in parties—in fact, all-female and all-male parties are common. When parties meet each other, individuals exchange pant-hoots and greetings. Often two or more parties merge to form a larger subgroup at a desirable location, such as a water source or tree loaded with ripe fruit. In one study, Jane Goodall and her partner observed 498 parties of common chimps. Forty-four percent of these parties had only two to four animals: females and their young. Only one percent of them had more than twenty individuals.

Bonobo parties typically have between two and fifteen animals, although parties as large as forty have been documented. Most bonobo parties are mixed, containing adult males, females, and offspring of all ages. Bonobos tend to remain in parties longer than common chimps do.

Parties and families often overlap, but they are not the same thing. Family relationships influence parties very differently among common chimpanzees and bonobos. Female common chimps often remain associated with their mothers throughout life, and their connections form the basis of many parties. Still, some females not only leave their mothers but their entire communities, joining other communities. Some later return to their birth communities. Among bonobos, however, all young females leave their communities, never to return. Bonobo parties tend to be organized around several friendly but unrelated adult females and their sons; sons remain associated with their mothers throughout adulthood.

Every community of common chimpanzees has a dominance hierarchy, headed by the top-ranking male. He may not be the biggest and strongest fellow around—the key to his dominance is not the ability to beat rivals in physical combat but rather the amount of support he gets from other males. He establishes this base of support through aggressive actions such as charging displays, through the loyalty of his male siblings, and

BY STANDING AND SHOWING HIS TEETH, THE MALE CHIMPANZEE ON THE LEFT IS DISPLAYING, A TYPE OF BEHAVIOR THAT CAN SIGNAL ANGER, AGGRESSION, OR FEAR. HE COULD DISPLAY EVEN MORE FORCEFULLY BY STAMPING HIS FEET, POUNDING ON THE BRANCH WITH HIS HANDS, OR SHAKING BRANCHES.

through social interactions such as sharing food. The other adult males form their own hierarchy beneath him. Each of them dominates some of the other males in the community and is submissive to others. Individual positions in the hierarchy change over time. Even the lowliest adult male, however, is dominant over all the females, who have their own hierarchy. Every party or group of parties is led by the dominant animal present.

Bonobos also have hierarchies, but they are less aggressive than common chimps about establishing dominance. In addition, female bonobos sometimes have equal rank with males, and females are the leaders of parties.

Although female common chimps may move from community to community, and female bonobos always do so, males of both species typically spend their entire lives in their birth communities. Communities accept new females, especially adolescent females without young, but a harsh reception awaits male outsiders who wander into their range. These intruders are hunted down and either chased away or attacked and killed. Adult males form parties to patrol the borders of their community's range, threatening any outsiders who approach. This type of aggressive territorial protection has been well documented among common chimpanzees. Bonobos, in contrast, tend to avoid encounters with parties from different communities. When such encounters do take place, the bonobos make noise, charge, and occasionally even fight, but they appear to be less violent than common chimps.

War, it seems, happens only among common chimpanzees. It takes several forms. In some cases, a larger or stronger community gradually wipes out a smaller or weaker one by moving into its home range. Some members of the weaker community flee. Over time, the newcomers kill the rest—except for adolescent females, who become part of their community. The other kind of conflict, called lethal raiding, occurs when parties of males invade another range with a deliberate plan to hunt and kill its inhabitants. The raiding parties sometimes carry weapons: stones for throwing and sticks for hitting. When they come upon a party from the other tribe, they overpower and kill its members, old and young, male and female—again, except for the adolescent females, whom they take back to their own territory. A third type of conflict occurs on rare occasions within a community, when a party of adult males attacks and kills other males of all ages. Some primatologists believe that these "civil wars" are triggered by overcrowding, which can occur if the community's population outgrows its resources or if its territory is reduced for some reason. Overcrowding seems to raise the levels of stress, aggression, and violent behavior in common chimpanzees.

Everyday Activities

At night chimpanzees sleep in tree nests. Each chimp (except for infants), makes its own nest. Chimps do not sleep in the same places every night, and each individual makes a new nest nearly every night. Once in a while chimps use old nests, including those made by other individuals. During the day, chimps frequently make smaller nests for naps or to rest out of the midday sun.

Although chimpanzees can move between closely spaced trees by climbing or leaping from branch to branch, common chimpanzees are more likely to climb down from one tree, walk across the ground to the next tree, and climb up into it. Bonobos are more active in the treetops and live only in fairly thick forest, but even they travel by ground from one group of trees to another. During a typical day, chimpanzees spend about half their time on the ground and half eating in the trees. Parties of animals move about, feeding in the morning, becoming less active in the middle of the day, and searching for food again in the afternoon. The average party covers a distance of about 1.5 miles (2.4 km) each day. One difference in the foraging patterns of the two species is that common chimpanzees dislike being wet. They go to great lengths to avoid possible soakings, and when they have to cross streams they show discomfort. Bonobos, in contrast, do not seem to fear the water or to mind getting wet. They frequently feed in swamps or along streams.

The diets of the two species differ as well. Common chimpanzees eat a very wide range of foods, depending upon habitat. On average, about 60 percent of a chimp's diet is fruit. Another 30 percent consists of leaves, flowers, seeds, nuts, bark, and honey. The final 10 percent is made up of animal foods, including insects (especially termites), larvae, or grubs; eggs; birds; rodents; and small mammals. When Jane Goodall began

A MALE CHIMPANZEE EATS FRUIT AT GOMBE NATIONAL PARK, ESTABLISHED ON THE SITE OF JANE GOODALL'S PIONEERING CHIMP RESEARCH IN TANZANIA. GOODALL NAMED THIS ANIMAL FRODO AND HAS DOCUMENTED MANY EVENTS OF HIS LIFE IN HER BOOKS.

her study of chimpanzees at Gombe Stream, zoologists thought chimpanzees were vegetarians. One of the biggest surprises of her early research was the discovery that chimps also hunt and kill animal prey. Since that time observers have documented their hunting methods. Males hunt more often than females, but any chimp can stalk and seize small prey. Larger prey animals—baboons, colobus monkeys, and young bushpigs—are generally brought down by a hunting party of males working together to chase or ambush the prey. The hunters share the meat. Other members of the community cluster around the kill, begging for pieces of meat, and the hunters may pass out tidbits. Common chimpanzees have been known to kill and eat at least a dozen species of monkeys—and, on occasion, other chimpanzees.

THE UPPER CHIMPANZEE HAS KILLED A BABOON, AND THE LOWER ONE IS BEGGING FOR A SHARE OF THE MEAT. ONE OF JANE GOODALL'S MOST STRIKING DISCOVERIES WAS EVIDENCE THAT CHIMPANZEES ARE HUNTERS AND MEAT-EATERS.

Bonobos occupy a narrower range of habitats than common chimps and have a slightly less varied diet. The balance of their diet is different, too. About 80 to 90 percent of it consists of fruit. The rest is leaves, seeds or nuts, and occasionally insects, earthworms, and small animals. Hunting for larger prey appears to be rare, although bonobos have been known to kill small duiker, a type of antelope.

A remarkable discovery about chimpanzees' use of plants began when a scientist named Richard Wrangham studied chimps at Gombe Stream in the 1970s. He noticed that some chimps occasionally sought out a type of plant called aspilia. They plucked leaves, held them in their mouths or rolled them around on their tongues for a few minutes, and then swallowed them whole—a very different method than the normal chewing. They did not seem to be eating aspilia for food because they consumed only a few leaves at a time. In the mid-1980s Wrangham got to know a plant chemist, whom he asked to analyze leaves of the aspilia plant. The chemist was surprised to discover that the leaves

ALTHOUGH GRASS IS NOT A MAJOR ITEM IN THE DIETS OF EITHER BONOBOS OR COMMON CHIMPANZEES, MANY ANIMALS DO CHEW ON GRASS FROM TIME TO TIME, PERHAPS AS A SNACK OR TO CLEAN THEIR TEETH.

contained a chemical called thiarubrine, previously known to exist only in roots. At almost the same time, Canadian scientists discovered thiarubine in a plant that Native Americans use in traditional medicines. Wrangham then learned that people in East Africa make many traditional medicines out of aspilia, the same plant eaten by the chimps. Since that time, laboratory research has found thiarubrine to be effective against fungi, parasitic worms, and some disease-causing bacteria and viruses. The chimpanzees at Gombe had apparently learned to use aspilia leaves as medicine. Field researchers later documented medicinal use of other plants by several chimpanzee communities.

When chimps are not sleeping or eating, they are likely to be grooming, a very important part of chimpanzee life. It reinforces connections between members of families, parties, and the entire community. During grooming, chimpanzees sit close together, often clucking or making soft hoots. One animal carefully picks through another's fur, removing bits of dirt and leaves as well as fleas and ticks. Grooming appears pleasurable, and it helps chimpanzees keep clean and free of parasites, but it is also a form of communication. Chimps ask to be groomed by presenting their backs to each other. A nervous or submissive chimp may present himself for grooming to a higher-ranking animal, seeking reassurance that the dominant chimp's attitude is friendly. Mother-child and sibling pairs spend long periods of time grooming one another, as do friendly pairs with long-standing bonds.

Chimpanzees can mate at any time of year, but they only do so when a female chimpanzee is in estrus, a period that occurs every thirty-six days. It lasts about a week, during which time she is receptive to males. Her readiness to mate is visible to all—the hairless skin around her sexual organs and rear end swells and becomes pink. If she mates but does not become pregnant, she will enter estrus again regularly until conception occurs. Once

GROOMING HELPS KEEP CHIMPS CLEAN AND FREE OF PARASITES. PERHAPS MORE IMPORTANTLY, IT STRENGTHENS BONDS AMONG INDIVIDUALS.

she becomes pregnant, she will not return to estrus for about five years, until after she has weaned her infant. If her infant dies before weaning, she will quickly return to estrus.

A female in estrus causes considerable excitement in a common chimpanzee community. Many of the males and even some of the females gather around her. Males try to impress her with special kinds of behavior called courtship displays. They include leaping around in the treetops, walking upright with stamping or swaggering steps, glaring, motioning for her to approach, and beating the ground with branches. (Some courtship behavior, as Goodall and others have noticed, is very similar to aggressive behavior.)

A FEMALE BONOBO WITH HER OFFSPRING. THE PINK SWELLING OF HER REAR END SHOWS THAT SHE HAS ENTERED ESTRUS AND IS NOW READY TO MATE AGAIN.

A JEALOUS MALE DISTURBS A PAIR OF MATING BONOBOS. FEMALE BONOBOS CHOOSE WHEN AND WITH WHOM THEY WILL MATE.

Chimpanzees have various patterns of mating behavior. Usually a female in estrus mates with many different males and they show little aggression toward each other. Sometimes, however, high-ranking males keep lower-ranking ones from mating with the females. Occasionally a male and female pair go off on their own, perhaps even leaving the community's home range entirely, to form a temporary relationship called a consortship. During consortship, the pair mate only with each other. The arrangement can last as long as three months and ends when the pair returns to the community. One form of sexual behavior has been observed in common chimps but not in bonobos. If a female in estrus is afraid or unwilling to mate, or if she refuses to accept a particular male, the male may force himself upon her— behavior that humans call rape. In general, among common chimps, males tend to control mating, while among bonobos, females choose when to mate and with whom.

Intelligence

Measuring the intelligence of animals—even animals as human-like as chimpanzees—is a difficult task. Because animals see the world differently from people and have different ways of life, some experts in animal behavior think that it is a mistake to try measuring their intelligence according to human standards. Chimpanzee and human brains are much alike, however, and many people who have studied and worked with chimps report constant amazement at the animals' cleverness.

Some primate researchers think that one sign of chimpanzees' high intelligence is their ability to fashion tools from objects around them. One of the first and most dramatic announcements to come out of Gombe was Jane Goodall's 1960 discovery that common chimpanzees use tools. Zoologists have long known that some animals make use of objects from the world in their search for food. Otters, for example, balance rocks on their stomachs as they float in the water, opening mussel shells by banging them against the rocks. Certain birds use cactus needles to probe into cracks in the bark of trees to look for insects. But no animal, scientists once thought, used tools in the way that humans do—making and modifying a variety of tools for specific purposes.

Tool use by chimpanzees was first documented when Goodall observed the chimp she called David Graybeard "fishing" for termites. He carefully selected a long grass stem, peeled away the leaves, bit off the end, and stuck the stem into a hole in a termite mound. When he pulled it out, it was covered with termites that had rushed to bite it. The chimp was able to eat the termites right off the stick, avoiding the messy process of digging into their mound and being painfully bitten. Goodall later recorded in great detail how chimps use stems and twigs to fish for both ants and termites, and how young chimps learn the process by watching experienced adults and copying them. Not all chimpanzee communities, however, practice fishing. It is now clear that this kind of tool use is not an instinctive behavior, which all chimps would do whether or not they saw other chimps performing it. Chimpanzees do not use items as they find them. They change the items to suit their purposes, thus creating and modifying tools. In addition, chimpanzee tool use is learned and passed from one generation to the next. It is an aspect of their culture.

Culture among wild chimpanzees varies from place to place. Some groups fish for ants and termites, while others use sticks to smash open termite mounds. In some parts of Africa, chimps use fishing sticks to draw honey from beehives. Elsewhere they break into beehives with sticks. The way they select and use tools

THESE UGANDAN CHIMPANZEES "FISH" FOR TERMITES WITH SLENDER STICKS. CHIMPS ALSO USE GRASS STEMS AS FISHING TOOLS AT TERMITE MOUNDS AND ANTHILLS.

differs as well. Some use grass stems for fishing, while others use sticks. Some groups of chimps have been observed using wads of leaves as sponges to soak up drinking water from puddles too shallow to drink from. Chimpanzees sometimes also use leaves as toilet paper or to wipe themselves clean of mud, blood, or sticky foods. The chimps of West Africa use tools in a way found nowhere else. To get at the meat found inside very hard nuts, they place a nut in a carefully selected resting place to hold it steady, such as a small hollow in a flat rock or hard tree root. Then they strike the nut with a rock chosen for its size, weight, and shape. Some of the striking rocks and resting places have been used by several generations of chimpanzees. Chimps have been seen carrying the striking rocks from one resting place to another. Common chimpanzees everywhere also use sticks and stones as weapons for both throwing and striking.

Scientists have not observed bonobos using tools in the wild. Captive individuals, however, have been known to use sticks for poking and leaves for wiping. And in a striking demonstration of chimpanzees' ability to learn new skills and solve problems, researchers have taught at least one bonobo to manufacture crude stone tools that are somewhat like those made by ancient human ancestors, although the chimpanzee's products are less sharp and well designed than those made by hominids.

Through teaching or simple experimenting, captive common chimps have learned to use many objects. They understand how mirrors work and use them to examine themselves. They also use mirrors to look at parts of their surroundings they cannot see directly. They use boards or poles as ladders and, if they get their hands on keys, they can open locks. A chimpanzee named Lucy, raised in isolation from other chimps and treated like a human child by her caretakers, learned to eat with silverware and to make tea.

Chimpanzees are also clever when it comes to getting what they want in social situations. They have been observed engaging in barter, both with each other and with humans, offering to trade something they don't particularly want, such as a stick or a piece of bread, for something they crave, such as a banana. If intelligence is defined as the ability to use tools and communication to control one's circumstances and satisfy one's needs,

CHIMPANZEES' HANDS ARE LARGER AND STRONGER THAN HUMAN HANDS. THEY MOVE IN MUCH THE SAME WAY AS HUMAN HANDS, HOWEVER. LIKE PEOPLE, CHIMPANZEES CAN MAKE CAREFUL, DELICATE MOVEMENTS WHEN MANIPULATING OBJECTS. THEY HAVE LEARNED TO TURN KEYS IN LOCKS, TO USE COMPUTER KEYBOARDS, AND TO DRAW AND PAINT.

chimpanzees seem to have more intelligence than any other nonhuman creatures.

Language

One attention-getting aspect of primate research concerns apes and language. In dozens of experimental programs, researchers have tried to teach human languages to gorillas, orangutans, and both species of chimpanzees. Results are uneven and in some cases hard to interpret. Much evidence, however, suggests that at least some apes possess unexpected language-using abilities.

The idea of communicating with apes is not new. Samuel Pepys, a seventeenth-century Englishman, saw a chimpanzee on display in London and wrote in his diary, "I do believe it already understands much englishe; and I am of the mind it might be taught to speak or make signs." In a 1925 book called *Almost Human*, primatologist Robert Yerkes declared that he believed that apes have "plenty to talk about" but could not develop complex and expressive spoken languages because the anatomy of their throats and mouths limits them to only a few vocalizations.

Researchers did manage to teach a chimpanzee called Vicki to utter a few words, but her speech was almost impossible to understand. Another approach was clearly needed. "Perhaps," wrote Yerkes, "they can be taught to use their fingers, somewhat as does the deaf and dumb person, and thus helped to acquire a simple, nonvocal, 'sign language.'"

In 1966 researchers put Yerkes's suggestion into practice. They began teaching American Sign Language, or ASL, to a young female common chimpanzee named Washoe. Within six years Washoe had learned 150 signs. Most of the signs Washoe used involved things that she liked, such as food, play, or tickling. The most surprising aspect of the project, though, was that a young male chimp named Loulis, whom Washoe treated as an adopted son, eventually began using ASL signs that no human trainer had ever used in his presence. He had learned them from Washoe.

Lucy, the chimp raised like a human child, learned more than a hundred signs and, without prompting, combined them in original ways to create new "words." For example, she called onions "cry fruit." Other chimpanzees have learned as many as 300 signs. A female gorilla named Koko has learned ASL and has been videotaped using sign language to talk to herself when she is alone, playing or looking at magazines. But ape-language

WASHOE, A FEMALE CHIMPANZEE WHO LEARNED TO COMMUNICATE WITH AMERICAN
SIGN LANGUAGE (ASL), IS ONE OF SEVERAL PRIMATES WHO HAVE HAD PET CATS.
CHIMPANZEES, LIKE HUMANS, SEEM TO HAVE BOTH THE DESIRE FOR COMPANIONSHIP
AND THE ABILITY TO FORM BONDS WITH OTHER SPECIES.

research has also produced failures and questions. One failure involved a chimpanzee named Nim, the subject of a research program at Columbia University in the 1970s. Although at first Nim seemed to be combining signs in original ways to express new concepts, review of the laboratory videotapes revealed that Nim's trainers had prompted much of his signing and that he was imitating them.

Ape-language research came in for harsh criticism during the late 1970s and the 1980s. Some scientists argued that apes who appeared to use language were really copying or playing with their trainers. Like dogs or horses, they gave their trainers the "right" responses by picking up on cues—such as rate of breathing or tone of voice—that the trainers did not even realize they were giving. Some language experts accepted the idea that apes might learn words, but they felt that the apes did not use language in the human sense to express their own ideas. They questioned whether apes could ever understand or use the key underlying structural features of human languages, such as using different verb forms to refer to past or future events, or differences between subjects (things that act) and objects (things that are acted on).

Researchers in Japan and the United States have been investigating these issues. They have learned from earlier failures and criticisms that their experiments must be carefully designed to reveal what chimpanzees really do, not what the experimenters think they can do or want them to do. One center of research is Georgia State University's Language Research Center, where a biologist and psychologist named Sue Savage-Rumbaugh has led a team studying the language abilities of bonobos. Instead of sign language, the chimpanzees "speak" through computers equipped with special keyboards bearing symbols instead of letters.

Dr. Sue Savage-Rumbaugh, a leading ape-language researcher, has achieved remarkable results in teaching bonobos to communicate by pointing to symbols that stand for words. She has developed special keyboards that feature the symbols in place of letters so that her research subjects can type their responses into a computer.

In *Kanzi: The Ape at the Brink of the Human Mind,* Savage-Rumbaugh describes some results of her ape-language research:

Kanzi has told us where he left a ball the day before and reminded us of yesterday's promise that we forgot. . . . Sherman told me there was a "scare" outdoors when he saw a chimp being carried away in a transport cage, and Austin always tells me he wants Coke instead of the juice I am offering. . . . Panbanisha tells me when it is raining outdoors. She also told me that the lady who visited has hair that looks like a mushroom—and she was really right. These are small things perhaps, but they offer a constant glimpse of other minds that I would not have without language.

6 Chimpanzees, Today and Tomorrow

Do chimpanzees deserve better treatment than other animals because they use tools and may use language—in short, because they are so much like us? How should we treat our closest relatives? Chimpanzees and the way humans act toward them are the focus of difficult questions. Controversy swirls around the use of chimps in medical experiments and the fate of captive chimps. The fate of wild chimps also hangs in the balance, shadowed by social and environmental crises in Africa.

Controversies

Since the 1920s, scientists in many parts of the world have experimented on chimpanzees. In some cases chimps have been stand-ins or substitutes for people. For example, in 1961 a chimpanzee

HAM THE CHIMPANZEE IS RELEASED FROM A *MERCURY* CAPSULE AFTER HIS 1961 SPACEFLIGHT. HAM SURVIVED THE TRIP INTO SPACE WITH NO ILL EFFECTS, LEADING SCIENTISTS TO BELIEVE THAT HUMANS COULD SURVIVE SPACEFLIGHT AS WELL

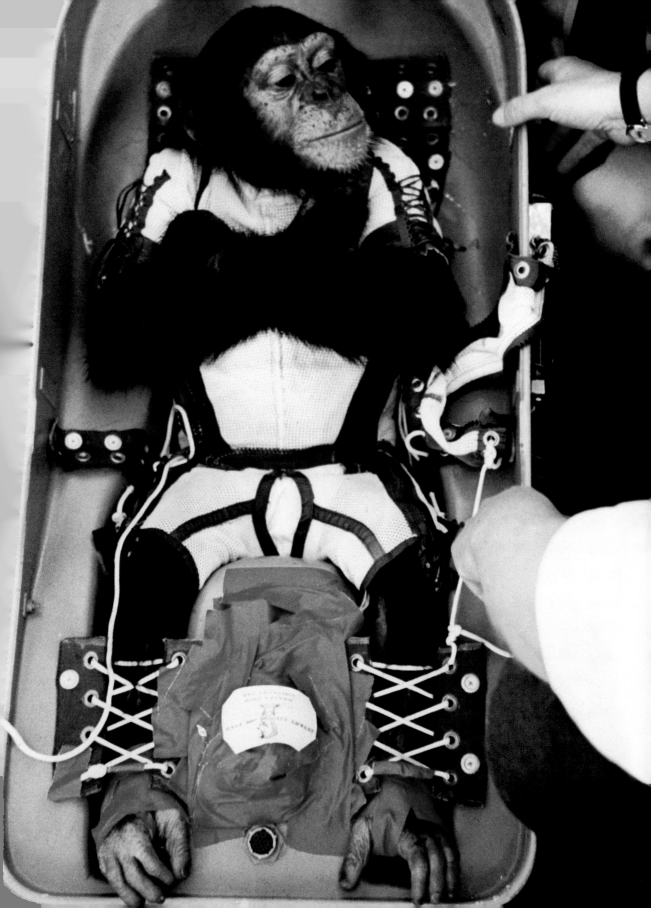

named Ham became an astronaut—the U.S. government sent him into space to see what effect the trip would have on his body before risking a human life. Many thousands more chimpanzees have been dissected, infected with diseases, or otherwise experimented on in the course of biological, medical, and psychological research.

In the early 1920s a scientist named Henry Nissen kept an infant chimpanzee's arms encased in plaster for two years. The animal was unable to touch itself or to move its arms. The idea was to see whether arm movements such as scratching were inborn or had to be learned. Not surprisingly, when the plaster came off, the little chimp's muscles were wasted and it could barely move its arms at all. The experiment not only didn't answer the question, but Jane Goodall has pointed out that it *couldn't* answer the question. It was simply a poorly designed and cruel waste of time. Perhaps the same is true of the "head-impact tolerance" experiments of the 1970s in which researchers at the U.S. National Institutes of Health fastened chimpanzees to metal frameworks. Pistons driven by compressed air then struck the chimps' heads, in some cases repeatedly, with forces of up to 4,000 pounds (1,814 kg). The chimps received no drugs to dull their pain or fear.

People for the Ethical Treatment of Animals (PETA) and other animal-welfare activism organizations argue that experiments going on today are equally cruel—or at least that they need better monitoring by outsiders. (The military, in particular, is not required to publish the details of research programs involving experimental animals, including chimpanzees.) One active area of research involves disease. Because chimpanzees share such a close genetic relationship with humans, some biomedical experts consider them excellent subjects for research into the causes and cures of human disease. Thousands of chimpanzees have been infected with dozens of diseases over the years. Some of these experiments have had outstanding results. Research on chimps led to a cure for a viral disease known as kuru, for example, and studies of chimpanzee brain function have helped scientists understand addiction.

DAVID SIDDLE, ONE OF THE FOUNDERS OF THE CHIMFUNSHI CHIMPANZEE REFUGE, HOLDS THREE YOUNG ORPHANS.

Other studies, however, have been less productive. When scientists learned that chimpanzees carry a form of HIV, the virus that causes AIDS in humans, they began costly, large-scale research projects, infecting thousands of chimps with HIV. None of these chimpanzees has ever become sick with AIDS. Experts now believe that chimps do not get this disease, although they do not know why they don't. These experiments produced chimps who are useless for further research but cannot be released to mingle with other chimpanzees because of the remote possibility that they might spread the virus.

A broad range of views exists about animal testing in general and chimpanzee testing in particular. The most extreme version of the animal-rights position says that all experimentation on any animal for any reason is wrong. Other people are against experiments that cause pain, injury, or illness to animals, but they support experiments that study animals' behavior without hurting them. Still others can accept the idea of experiments on animals such as rats, especially if they are aimed at saving human lives, but grow uncomfortable at the thought of chimpanzees in laboratories.

Apart from the question of the experiments themselves, there is also the issue of how the chimps are housed and treated. Many of them live in cramped, sterile, miserable conditions. Jane Goodall has done much to educate those who raise, house, and use primates for research about what chimpanzees need to maintain their physical and mental health. Some labs, breeding facilities, and captive-chimp colonies now house chimps in larger cages and enclosures and give them toys and other things, like magazines, to prevent boredom. Chimps in some facilities are even allowed to have social contact with each other. In the United States, the Animal Welfare Act requires laboratories using primates to have programs that enrich the animals'

ORPHANED CHIMPANZEES AT AN APE RESCUE CENTER IN ENGLAND. CENTERS IN MANY COUNTRIES CARE FOR ANIMALS RESCUED FROM THE ILLEGAL WILDLIFE TRADE.

environments and offer opportunities for normal behavior.

What happens to experimental chimpanzees when the experiments are over? Sometimes they are simply assigned to other research programs. Many, however, are killed, especially if they are too diseased, old, or ill-adjusted to be useful in another program. Concerned individuals and primate-protection organizations have founded some sanctuaries to take in these and other cast-off chimps, but more such refuges are needed. In 2002 the U.S. government announced that it would pay $8 million toward the $14-million cost of a refuge for aging chimps from research or entertainment backgrounds.

"IF CHIMPANZEES KNEW FULLY WHAT WE ARE DOING TO THEM, AND IF THEY HAD THE CAPACITY TO SPEAK, WHAT WOULD THEY SAY?" WROTE DALE PETERSON IN *VISIONS OF CALIBAN*, A BOOK ABOUT HUMAN TREATMENT OF CHIMPANZEES.

The question of how we should treat captive chimpanzees will only become more troubling and complicated if, as many primatologists expect, we continue to discover things that chimps and humans have in common. Writes Dale Peterson in *Visions of Caliban*, "If chimpanzees knew fully what we are doing to them, and if they had the capacity to speak, what would they say?"

Conservation

Chimpanzees in captivity give rise to questions about how they are to be used and treated. The question concerning wild chimpanzees is one of simple survival. Both common chimpanzees and bonobos are recognized as endangered species by the U.S. government and the International Union for the Conservation of Nature and Natural Resources (IUCN).

Estimates of the total number of chimpanzees remaining in the wild at the beginning of the twenty-first century range from 150,000 to 250,000, down from several million a century ago. Some chimpanzees have been lost to the wild-animal trade. Hunters seeking to capture live chimpanzees for sale cannot usually control adults, so they kill the adults in a party and seize the infants. Several adult and adolescent chimps may die for every chimp captured. The most serious threats to chimpanzees, however, are habitat loss and bushmeat hunting.

Habitat loss occurs when a natural environment is changed in ways that make it difficult or impossible for wildlife to survive in it. Animals that require forest habitats, such as bonobos, are killed or displaced when forests are cut down for timber or to open up land for farming. Africa's tropical forests are being cut down at the rate of 110,000 acres (44,500 hectares) a year, according to the World Wildlife Federation. Savanna habitat is also being lost to cattle-grazing and farming.

Timber companies and local governments build roads into forested areas that are ready for logging. The roads carry more than loggers and trucks—they also carry poachers into newly opened areas. Africa is seeing a dramatic increase in the hunting, sale, and consumption of meat from wild animals, including chimpanzees, which some people consider a delicacy. Bushmeat, as it is called, has long been eaten for survival in rural villages, but now it is becoming a major food novelty in cities, where consumers are willing to pay higher prices for it than for meat from farm animals. About a million tons of bushmeat are taken out of the forests each year in the Congo River Basin alone, six times more than the wildlife population can replace. Janet Larsen of the Earth Policy Institute wrote in 2002, "Almost half of the 30 million people living in the forested regions of Africa are city-dwellers who are being fed with bushmeat from collapsing wildlife populations. As cities grow and bushmeat hunting accelerates to meet rising demand, it is estimated that hunting could eliminate all viable ape populations in fewer than twenty years."

Most countries where chimpanzees live have made it illegal to kill, capture, or sell them, but the laws are often ignored or poorly enforced. The safest places for chimpanzees are the various national parks and wildlife reserves scattered across tropical Africa, but even in protected zones chimpanzees are not safe from poachers, or hunters who hunt illegally. Two steps that will be necessary if chimpanzees are to be truly protected are, first, cracking down on the illegal trade in live chimps and chimpanzee bushmeat and, second, building sanctuaries for injured or orphaned chimps that cannot be returned to the wild. Some such sanctuaries already exist. As centers of education about primates and sources of income from tourism, they contribute to local economies and to regional conservation efforts.

The threat to chimpanzees' survival is just part of the great

A CHIMPANZEE'S PAW GRASPING ITS CAGE.

crisis facing the tropical forests of Africa, where war, poverty, and the need for economic development often stand in the way of conservation efforts. Environmental biologists hope, however, that by creating a network of preserves across the center of the continent and providing local governments with the training and funds to manage and police them properly, conservationists may manage to save some of this extraordinary habitat and its diverse wildlife. Says Jane Goodall, guiding spirit of chimpanzee studies and the chimps' most passionate defender, "Chimpanzees—at least some chimpanzees—will survive if humans choose that they do so." If chimpanzees do not survive, human beings will be alone in a new way, having lost the closest link to their origins in the natural world.

Glossary

adapt—to change or develop in ways that aid survival in the environment

ancestral—having to do with lines of descent or earlier forms

anthropoid—an ape

arboreal—living in trees

bipedal—on two feet

conservation—action or movement aimed at saving or preserving wildlife or its habitat

diurnal—active by day

evolution—the process by which new species, or types of plants and animals, emerge from old ones over time

evolve—to change over time

extinct—no longer existing; having died out

forage—to look for food

genetic—material made of DNA inside the cells of living organisms. Genes determine the particular characteristics of an organism

habitat—type of environment in which an animal lives

hominids—manlike primates, limited to humans and their direct ancestors

hominoids—the group of primates that includes humans and apes and their shared ancestors

mammal—animal with a backbone that nourishes its young with milk from its mammary glands. All primates are mammals, as are thousands of other animals, from mice to whales.

nocturnal—active by night

organism—any living thing

paleontology—the study of ancient or extinct life-forms, usually through fossils

primate—any member of the group of mammals that includes prosimians, monkeys, apes, and humans

primatologist—a scientist who specializes in the study of primates

savanna—tropical or subtropical grassland with scattered trees or patches of woodland

simian—a monkey or ape, or characteristic of monkeys or apes

taxonomy—a scientific system for classifying living things, arranging them in categories according to similarities and differences, and naming them

zoologist—a scientist who specializes in the study of animals

Species Checklist

Two species and three subspecies of chimpanzees live in the world today. The list below gives their scientific and common names and tells where they live. (Chimpanzeelike animals recently found in the Democratic Republic of Congo may represent a fourth subspecies of *Pan troglodytes*, or possibly a new species of primate. They have not yet been classified.)

Scientific name	Common name	Range
Pan paniscus	Bonobo (formerly called pygmy chimpanzee)	Democratic Republic of Congo
Pan troglodytes	Common chimpanzee	
• *P. troglodytes schweinfurthii*	Eastern chimpanzee	Eastern Africa
• *P. troglodytes troglodytes*	Central chimpanzee	Central and west-central Africa
• *P. troglodytes verus*	Western chimpanzee	West Africa

Further Research

Books for Young People

Banks, Martin. *Chimpanzee: Habitats, Life Cycles, Food Chains, Threats.* Austin, TX: Raintree Steck-Vaughn, 2000.

Constable, Tamsin. *Chimpanzees: Social Climbers of the Forest.* New York: Dorling Kindersley, 2001.

Goodall, Jane. *Jane Goodall's Animal World: Chimps.* New York: London: Aladdin Books; Collier Macmillan, 1989.

————. *The Chimpanzees I Love: Saving Their World and Ours.* New York: Scholastic, 2001.

Redmond, Ian. *Gorilla, Monkey & Ape.* New York: Dorling Kindersley, 2000.

Saign, Geoffrey. *The Great Apes.* New York: Franklin Watts, 1998.

Stonehouse, Bernard. *A Visual Introduction to Monkeys and Apes.* New York: Checkmark Books, 1999.

Videos

Among the Wild Chimpanzees. National Geographic Video, 1987.

Chimps: So Like Us. Direct Cinema Ltd., 1991.

Jane Goodall: My Life with the Chimpanzees. National Geographic Video, 1995.

Pan troglodytes: An In-Depth Study. PBS Video, 1996.

Search for the Great Apes. National Geographic Video, 1995.

Web Sites

http://www.janegoodall.org
> The official Web site of the Jane Goodall Institute includes a biography of the scientist, an overview of her chimpanzee research, and information about chimps.

http://www.gsu.edu/~wwwlrc
> The Web site of the Language Research Center at Georgia State University, where psychologists study the language-using abilities of chimpanzees such as Kanzi, describes the center's work and has links to other primate Web sites.

http://www.oaklandzoo.org/atoz/azchimp.html
> The Oakland Zoo's Web site includes this page of general information about chimpanzees, with a list of recommended reading.

http://www.emory.edu/YERKES
> The Yerkes National Primate Research Center maintains this Web site as a source of information about its research programs and about primate conservation.

http://www.primate.wisc.edu/pin
> The University of Wisconsin's Primate Research Center operates the Primate Information Network, an online source of scientific and conservation information that includes information about chimpanzees and links to may other Web sites.

http://www.indiana.edu/~primate/primates.html
> The African Primates at Home site features information about African primates along with scenes and sounds of them in natural settings.

http://www.cwu.edu/~cwuchci
> The Web site of the Chimpanzee and Human Communication Institute at Central Washington University, home of the signing chimp Washoe, includes material about chimps for students, along with biographies of Washoe and other chimps.

http://www.ippl.org
> The home page of the International Primate Protection League, which has worked since 1973 to protect primates around the world from poaching, habitat loss, and other threats.

http://www.aza.org
> The American Zoo and Aquarium Association offers guidelines for managing captive animals and a detailed species survival plan for chimpanzees.

Bibliography

The author found these books especially helpful when researching this volume.

Fleagle, John. *Primate Adaptation and Evolution*. 2nd ed. San Diego: Academic Press, 1999.
     Overview of discoveries and theories in the field of primate evolution.
Ghiglieri, Michael. *East of the Mountains of the Moon: Chimpanzee Society in the African Rain Forest*. New York: Free Press, 1988.
     Description of the lives and social behavior of forest chimps.
Goodall, Jane. *The Chimpanzees of Gombe: Patterns of Behavior*. Cambridge, MA: Harvard University Press, 1986.
     A study of chimpanzee behavior in the wild, with emphasis on their social structures.
——————. *In the Shadow of Man*. Rev. ed. Boston: Houghton Mifflin, 1988.
     Originally published 1971. One of Goodall's best-known works on chimpanzees, illustrated with photographs of them in natural settings.
Heltne, Paul and Linda Marquardt, eds. *Understanding Chimpanzees*. Cambridge, MA: Harvard University Press, 1989.
     Essays on various aspects of chimpanzee studies.
Peterson, Dale. *Chimpanzee Travels: On and Off the Road in Africa*. Reading, MA: Addison-Wesley, 1995.
     Account of fieldwork on chimpanzees in Africa.
Peterson, Dale, and Jane Goodall. *Visions of Caliban: On Chimpanzees and People*. Boston: Houghton Mifflin, 1993.
     Covers the subject of human-chimpanzee relationships.
Savage-Rumbaugh, Sue. *Kanzi: The Ape at the Brink of the Human Mind*. New York: John Wiley and Sons, 1994.
     Reports on studies of learning and communication by studying a bonobo.
Siddle, Sheila. *In My Family Tree: A Life with Chimpanzees*. New York: Grove Press, 2002.
Wrangham, Richard W., ed. *Chimpanzee Cultures*. Cambridge, MA: Harvard University Press in association with the Chicago Academy of Sciences, 1994.
     Essays on behavior, ecology, and intelligence in bonobos and chimpanzees.

Index

Page numbers in **boldface** are illustrations.

About the Author

REBECCA STEFOFF has written many books on scientific and historical subjects for children and young adults. Among her other books on animal life are *Horses* (honored by the American Society for the Prevention of Cruelty to Animals for promoting a better understanding of the relationship between people and animals), *Bears*, *Tigers*, *Dogs*, and *Cats* in Marshall Cavendish's AnimalWays series and the eighteen volumes of the Living Things series, also published by Benchmark Books. Stefoff lives in Portland, Oregon.